0-60
IN 120
YEARS

0-60
IN 120
YEARS

A TIMELINE OF BRITISH MOTORING

KEITH RAY

The
History
Press

First published 2014

The History Press
The Mill, Brimscombe Port
Stroud, Gloucestershire, GL5 2QG
www.thehistorypress.co.uk

British Library Cataloguing in Publication Data.
A catalogue record for this book is available from the British Library.

ISBN 978 0 7524 9757 0

Typesetting and origination by The History Press
Printed in India

Contents

Introduction

I've called this book *0–60 in 120 Years* because 120, apart from being a rather nice-sounding round number, is also the number of years which separate the introduction of the 'Red Flag' in 1865 from the completion of the M25 in 1985. Of course, British motoring didn't start with the introduction of the Red Flag, nor did it finish with the opening of the M25, but these two events are notable milestones in the evolution of motoring as we know it today. The first – the introduction of legislation requiring a man with a red flag to walk in front of every motorised vehicle – saw the beginning of ever increasing legal restrictions on the motorist. The second – the opening of the M25 – was intended to be a liberating influence. However, it turned out to be so successful, and eventually so congested, that it has effectively become Europe's longest car park; indeed, we should remember that the Abercrombie Plan for transport in London published in 1944 recommended not one but five ring motorways for London – hardly surprising then that the lone M25 is now overcrowded. In that sense, things have come full circle and we have inadvertently imposed new restrictions on the poor motorist through the car being so popular.

0–60 in 120 Years takes you on a journey from the days in Britain when the very first mechanised, self-propelled vehicles appeared, to the present day. It looks not only at the vehicles themselves but also at the evolution of the infrastructure we drive along, the changes in legislation – sometimes for the better, but usually for the worse – as well as some of the social aspects of improved mobility. It also briefly delves into transport in Britain before self-propelled vehicles appeared, as some of the 'pre-history' events still have a bearing on how we move around the country today.

This book is organised around a timeline, which, after the 'pre-history' section, has been divided into separate decades. Within each decade section the major events are presented year by year. In addition, at the beginning of each decade, there is a summary of the major changes in the automobile industry, and throughout the book a number of features which cut across time, for example a summary of changes in legal speed limits since the motor car first appeared. There are also profiles of some of the cars which have become iconic of their age.

Reviewing how things have changed over the last 120-plus years, it is interesting to ponder over what the next century on the roads will bring. Will we even have roads and motor cars? Considering the fact that in 1865, 4mph in open country and 2mph in towns were considered the maximum safe speed, and that today most family cars will easily exceed 100mph safely – although not legally – speculating about the future might seem futile. Maybe we'll have 400mph cars which can drive themselves, and also fly, travel on water, produce no pollution at all and maybe, just maybe, also do the ironing and washing up. Who knows? Having said that, many motorists in London would be very happy to be able to travel today at even the 2mph seen as the safe maximum in 1865!

Let's start with an insightful quote from Bill Gates: 'If GM had kept up with technology like the computer industry has, we would all be driving $25 cars that got 1,000mpg.' A nice dream, perhaps. In reality, cars have hardly changed at all in price in real terms since 1920, but they have become much more sophisticated and offer much more to the motorist than they used to.

Finally, an anonymous author wrote: 'Money can't buy happiness – but somehow it's more comforting to cry in a Rolls Royce than a Ford.' Who can argue with that? Especially if they've also bought this book!

Leading up to the Automobile

In the years leading up to the motor car there was a lot of activity around horse-drawn and steam-driven vehicles, which was much more 'public' transport than private. It would take the petrol-driven motor car to liberate people at an individual level just as the nineteenth century was coming to an end.

THE COST OF ROAD TRAVEL IN THE EIGHTEENTH CENTURY

We all like to complain about the cost of travel, whether by rail or by car, and in particular about the cost of petrol, which seems to rise inexorably. However, it is interesting to look back to the days before cars, buses and trains and look at the cost of travel then, especially in the eighteenth century, which was the heyday of coach travel. It is sobering to put those costs into today's money by adjusting for the Retail Price Index.

Whilst there appears to be no comprehensive review of changing travel costs over the ages, research has revealed some interesting facts. In each case the equivalent cost today is shown in brackets:

- In 1722 a survey by one William Stow about transport in London finds that the typical hackney carriage costs 10s (£78) per day, or 1s 6d (£10.50) per hour.
- In 1753 the Birmingham Stage Chaise leaves Birmingham every Monday, Wednesday and Friday for the 30-mile trip to Worcester, which takes five hours and costs 9s (£70) inside the coach or 5s (£39) outside, one way. It returns to Birmingham on Tuesdays, Thursdays and Saturdays.
- In the 1750s a certain Count Kielmansegg hires a landau in London to take him around England. It costs him 27s (£215) per day, whilst a German lady called Sophia de la Roche hires a carriage with two horses and a coachman for 15s (£119) per day. To put these into perspective, at

around the same time, the rent on a terraced London house suitable for a senior clerk, his family and one servant is typically around 38s a week.

- Also in the 1750s the typical stagecoach fare is 2d–3d (£1.35–£2.03) per mile.
- In 1784 the London to Bristol mail coach, which takes sixteen hours of discomfort, carries four inside passengers paying a one-way fare of 28s (£156).
- In 1790 the Highflyer coach from London to York, one way, costs £2 10s (£268) inside and £1 11s 6d (£168) outside. By contrast the quicker, but not really any more comfortable, Royal Mail coach from London to York cost £3 3s (£337) inside – almost a month's income for a teacher or vicar at the time.

But these basic fares were not the end of the matter at all! In addition to the basic fare, rather like with Ryanair, the traveller ended up having to pay many extras, including tips for the guards and coachmen, as well as paying for food and lodging on a journey that could take several days. Sir Walter Scott, when travelling from Edinburgh to London, reckoned he spent nine times the basic fare on these extras, taking the today's equivalent total cost of an Edinburgh to London journey up from around £700 for the basic fare to something like £7,000 all in!

Travel in the eighteeth century was strictly for the very rich. Most people only went as far as they could walk. The railways, and then the motor car, came along as true liberating influences for the mass of the population.

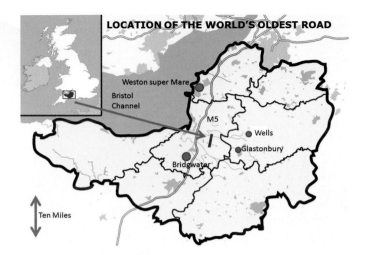

LOCATION OF THE WORLD'S OLDEST ROAD

Weston super Mare

Bristol Channel

M5

Wells

Glastonbury

Bridgwater

Ten Miles

3807 BC Britain can proudly lay claim to the oldest road in the world: the so-called 'Sweet Track' is an ancient causeway on the Somerset Levels, discovered in 1970, that has been dated by tree-ring dating to between winter 3807 BC and spring 3806 BC – you can't get much more precise than that! However, in 2009 an even older road, 6000 years old, was discovered in Plumstead near Belmarsh Prison – maybe it was advanced planning for a get-away route for future prisoners – but then it was subsequently discovered that the Sweet Track itself had been built over an even older road, the 'Post Track'. Whether Sweet Track, the Plumstead get-away route or the Post Track is the oldest, there has never been a road older than any of those three discovered anywhere on Earth. The only downside is that many residents in the Somerset Levels and the Plumstead area don't think their roads have improved materially since. That's a bit of a deviation from vehicle transport, but interesting nonetheless. Now, to get back on 'track' …

1300s The word 'car' first appears in the 1300s to describe a horse-drawn vehicle. It is said to derive originally from a Celtic word that sounded like 'karra' and which Julius Cesar used to describe his chariots, 'latinising' it to *carra*. After 1300 it evolved into the word 'carriage', from which it then later evolved back to 'car' once the horses had disappeared. So in theory the 'car' is over 700 years old – a bit like my first car felt.

1500s During the sixteenth century the stagecoach is first developed, enabling those who are rich enough to travel further than they could walk, and without the discomfort of horseback riding. This was the first organised road transport in Britain, and the first time roads had had to be more than simple muddy footpaths or bridle-ways.

1625 Hackney carriages start operating in London at the beginning of the seventeenth century and by 1625 there are twenty operating in London. Incidentally, the term 'Hackney' has nothing to do with the London borough of that name. It derives from the Norman French word *hacquenée*, meaning a type of horse suitable for hire, and covers a range of horse-drawn vehicles.

1635 Postal delivery services begin with mail carried on horseback, the postal service marking the beginning of the need for country-wide travel by road. However, it was very unsafe and inefficient and it would be 1784 before safer, more reliable mail coach services started. With these early mails it was the recipient who paid. It was not until the 'London Penny Post' in 1680 and the national 'Penny Post' in 1840 that the sender paid.

1636 The number of hackney carriages in London is limited to fifty to avoid cut-throat competition, possibly the first piece of road legislation in the country, and maybe the world. What a shame it wasn't the last! This year also sees the first 'taxi stand' set up in the Strand outside the Maypole Inn, although the term 'taxi' was not to be invented until 1907. Maybe they just called it the 'Strand Stand'.

1654 The regulations on hackney carriages are formalised in the 'Ordnance for the Regulation of hackney carriages in London and the Places Adjacent'. More regulation, and surely an ominous sign of things to come. The same year Oliver Cromwell sets up the Fellowship of Master hackney carriages by Act of Parliament and taxi driving becomes a 'profession'. This makes the licensed taxi trade in London the oldest regulated public transport system in the world, but not the oldest 'profession'.

A hackney carriage from around 1860, although little has changed since the seventeenth century. Indeed, many early nineteenth-century hackney carriages were actually second-hand eighteenth-century gentlemen's coaches, like the one in the picture. I'm not too sure about the coachman's hand signal, though.

The Verbiest steam vehicle.

1662 The first hackney carriage Licences in London are issued – the first licences associated with movement by road anywhere in the world. The same basic licence for black cabs continues to this day. Black cabs are still technically known as hackney carriages, meaning they may pick up fares on the street, as opposed to minicabs which have to be pre-booked. Of course, today they are neither 'Hackneys', meaning horse-drawn, nor, in many cases, even black!

1672 Although not British, it is worth noting that Ferdinand Verbiest, a Flemish member of a Jesuit mission in China, may have been the first person, or even parson, to build a self-propelled mechanical vehicle – a steam-powered creation built to entertain the Chinese emperor. Verbiest's claim to be the first builder of a 'motor vehicle' has two slight weaknesses, however: firstly, it was too small to carry passengers; secondly, and more importantly, there is little evidence it ever actually existed. If it could be proven, it would certainly elevate him to the ranks of famous Belgians – ranks which are pretty slimly populated, it must be said.

1708 The world's first recorded instance of a street being numbered is Prescot Street in Goodmans Fields, London, in 1708. By the end of the century, the numbering of houses had become well established and seems to have been done on the consecutive rather than the odd and even principle with which we have now become familiar.

1765 The Postage Act 1765 begins the process of nationally numbering houses on streets and roads, an early step in making navigation by road easier. When your satnav asks you to enter the house number, remember this eighteenth-century Act.

1769 Some sources, mainly French ones, claim Frenchman Nicolas-Joseph Cugnot built the first self-propelled mechanical vehicle. Well, he did build something that moved, although it gave a new slant to the meaning of the word 'move'. With a large boiler slung way out in front it was completely unstable; furthermore, the fire for the boiler needed to be cleaned out and relit and new steam raised again from cold every fifteen minutes, so progress would have made a geriatric snail look like Usain Bolt! Not surprisingly, it came to nothing – apart from demolishing a few walls, as it was almost impossible to steer.

The Cugnot, built by Frenchman Nicolas-Joseph Cygnot.

1771 Driving on the left and the delineation of the road with 'offside' and 'nearside' is enshrined in Scottish law, ahead of England. Rumours that the canny Scots sold the law to England are completely unfounded.

1784 Royal Mail stagecoaches were introduced on the order of William Pitt, Chancellor of the Exchequer, and a mail coach would make the 120-mile journey from London to Bristol in seventeen hours. Previously, mail carried by a single horse and rider took thirty-eight hours including resting time.

1785 William Pitt increases Royal Mail services from London to eleven more English cities, and to Edinburgh the following year.

1801 The real prize for the first successful 'motor vehicle' must go to Cornishman Richard Trevithick. His steam-powered motor vehicle could carry eight passengers, which he demonstrated by driving through Camborne, fully laden, at a breath-taking average speed of 8.4mph, marginally faster than a mail coach. So I think in fairness to Trevithick we can say 'Great Britain 1, France 0'. Incidentally, 'fast' is probably the best way to drive through Camborne, as there really isn't much to see.

1803 Buoyed by his success in Cornwall, Trevithick then builds a second carriage and takes it to London where it makes several successful runs, achieving the dizzying speed of 10mph. Unfortunately it also frightens horses and receives much hostility from the public who, in the absence of cars, do rely somewhat on the horse. As a result he is unable to gain any further backing and his carriage is dismantled in 1804.

1807 The world's first passenger tram service, drawn by two horses, starts between Mumbles and Swansea in South Wales.

1810 An attempt is made to bore a tram tunnel under the River Severn to take road traffic, but it is abandoned after 138yd because of flooding. Did nobody tell them rivers are rather wet things?

The first steam-powered motor vehicle. (Courtesy of Chris Allen)

An accurate replica of Richard Trevithicks's coach. (Courtesy of Barry Herbert)

Left: It appears from this ancient photograph that the Mumbles tram could carry around fifty people. The photograph dates from around 1839, when photography was invented, so the service must have been a success to survive at least thirty-two years.

Dating from before 1890, when side arches for pedestrians were added, this is perhaps the only surviving photograph of Nash's original arch.

Reigate Tunnel.

1813 Archway Road in North London becomes, arguably, the country's, and maybe the world's, first true bypass. Built to avoid congestion in the village of Highgate, already a snobby enclave by 1813, and make the climb up the hill easier for the horses, it had originally been planned as a tunnel, but this collapsed and instead the cutting we know today was dug out. The first 'archway' was built by John Nash, but when the Highgate bypass was widened in 1897 this was replaced by the present iron arch which carries the Hornsey Road. This newer arch is unfortunately perhaps best known for the number of suicides it has witnessed.

1823 The world's first road tunnel is built in Reigate. It was constructed and paid for by Earl Sommers, who owned a house on the top of the hill and wanted to stop traffic passing through his grounds, an early example of 'Nimbyism'. Until 1856 it levied a toll of ½d for a horse and 6d for a coach and four horses. Pedestrians could go for free. Up to the 1970s it was still used by road traffic as part of the A217, causing a bottleneck of biblical proportions.

1824 Timothy Burstall and John Hill build a four-wheel-drive steam coach in London, which weighs 7 tons and is capable of 4mph. Well, it was capable of 4mph for the brief time it ran before shaking itself to pieces on the dreadful road surfaces of the day. It looked exactly like a horse-drawn coach without the horses – mainly because it *was* a horse-drawn coach without the horses, simply modified with a steam engine hanging out at the front.

1826 Samuel Brown becomes the first person to build a vehicle powered by an internal combustion engine. His patented 'gas and vacuum' engine works by using a gas flame to expel the air from a chamber and then using the air sucked back in to power a twin-cylinder engine. It is similar in concept to Watt's condensing steam engine but without the steam. With a nominal 8.8-litre capacity it generated just 4bhp, which works out at a staggering 0.45bhp per litre. Installed in a coach, however, it makes successful demonstration runs up Shooters Hill in London. Nonetheless, his design was too expensive to ever be commercially viable.

1829 Sir Goldsworthy Gurney, a true Victorian polymath and another Cornishman, builds several steam carriages between 1825 and 1829 and is the first person to seriously consider the commercialisation of mechanised road transport.

On trial runs around north London his coaches prove capable of 20mph – faster than most London buses are able to travel today! By 1829 his designs are robust enough to undertake the world's first long-distance coach service, a round trip from London to Bath and back. However, it meets with hostility and is not commercially viable.

1830 Walter Hancock sets up a regular omnibus service in London between Stratford and Paddington using *Infant*, his second steam carriage, and it is the first regular motorised bus service in the world. The same omnibus was later used on a much longer scheduled service to Brighton.

1831 Sir Charles Dance creates what was, in many ways, the first proper bus company, running several of Gurney's steam coaches over a number of routes, including Gloucester to Cheltenham, London to Brighton, and Wellington Street to Greenwich in London.

Gurney's steam carriage.

1833 Walter Hancock starts a scheduled steam coach service between Paddington and Regents Park. His new coach, *The Enterprise*, takes fourteen passengers and the fare is *6d* per head (£2.25 in today's money, about the same as an Underground Zone 1 fare). It is both the first properly scheduled bus service, and the first vehicle specifically designed as a bus, in the world.

A replica of *Enterprise*. (Courtesy of Barry Herbert)

1834 The expression 'hansom cab' appears for the first time. The hansom cab, invented by Joseph Aloysius Hansom (1803–82), displaces the hackney carriage for being faster, safer and cheaper to run. Most hackney carriages had four wheels, many being second-hand gentlemen's coaches, whereas the Hansom had just two wheels and the driver sat up high behind the enclosed cab (which is short for cabriolet). The hansom cab is the vehicle we associate with the London of Sherlock Holmes and Jack the Ripper.

1835 A Mr Church builds a three-wheeled steam omnibus capable of carrying forty-four passengers – twenty-two inside and twenty-two outside – for the London & Birmingham Steam Carriage Company, running on a route from London to Birmingham at an average speed of 14mph. The service was a great success until legislation limited the speed of coaches. It was one of the ugliest and most ungainly vehicles ever to move on British roads and it may be significant that, unlike Gurney's and Trevithick's vehicles, nobody has built a replica of Church's monstrosity.

This contemporary caricature of steam travel shows that public response is less than favourable.

Church's Coach. Possibly the ugliest wheeled vehicle of all time.

1835 It becomes mandatory to drive on the left side of the road, passing oncoming traffic right side to right side. This rule is believed to derive from coach drivers' desire to pass 'right to right' to facilitate the use of hand guns by the predominantly right-handed crew. However, in big cities, the congestion of horse-drawn traffic combined with the occasional steam coach results in more of a free-for-all as far as road discipline goes.

1836 A Parliamentary Commission of Enquiry reports 'strongly in favour of steam carriages on roads', although subsequent Acts of Parliament have tended to have a discouraging and restrictive effect on the development of road transport generally.

1840 The first mechanical vehicle travels more than 100 miles without breaking down. A steam carriage built by Francis Hill travels from London to Hastings and back without incident, demonstrating that motorised transport was not just for local journeys. Hill was indeed fortunate not to breakdown, as there was no AA, RAC or Green Flag in those days.

1843 It becomes compulsory for London cabmen to wear a metal badge showing their licence number so the public may identify them if needed, which they still do to this day.

1845 Robert William Thomson patents the world's first vulcanised rubber pneumatic tyre, but it does not reach production. Thomson is frustrated by the lack of suitable thin rubber and instead turned his attention to solid rubber tyres. It would not be until forty-three years later that the pneumatic tyre would become a practical reality when it was 'reinvented' by fellow Scot John Boyd Dunlop for use, at first, on bicycles.

1846 Modern Portland cement is invented by Joseph Aspidin, a Wakefield bricklayer, and he quickly applies it to road construction. An existing surface of wooden blocks set in lime cement on the Strand in London is removed and replaced by stone setts placed in Portland cement concrete, the very first use of modern concrete for roads.

1855 House numbering first becomes regulated in London with the passing of the Metropolitan Management Act. For the first time the power to control and regulate the naming and numbering of streets and houses is provided for and given to the new Board of Works. Under pressure from the Post Office the Board starts work in

1857 on the simplification of street names and numbering by working through a hit list of the most confusing streets given to the Board by the Post Office. This regulation will play an important part in how we move around towns and cities.

1861 The Locomotive Act 1861 is the first sign of what would become increasing regulation and restrictions on road use. The Act limits the weight of steam engines to 12 tons and imposes a blanket speed limit of 10mph.

1865 More bad news for road users in 1865. The Highways and Locomotives Act 1865 sets a speed limit for motorised vehicles of 4mph in the country and 2mph in towns. The Act also requires the 'man with the red flag' to walk 60yd ahead of each vehicle with a red flag or lantern to enforce a walking pace and warn horse riders and horse-drawn traffic of the approach of a self-propelled machine.

■Also in 1865, Joseph Mitchell, a student of Thomas Telford, experiments with Portland cement applied over a Macadam base, with the concrete allowed to penetrate the voids. He conducts two trials that year: one a 45m stretch of road near Inverness Station; and second a 100m stretch in St James's Park in London. These are the world's first concrete-surfaced roads.

1869 The world's first ever set of traffic lights is installed outside the Houses of Parliament by J.P. Knight, a railway engineer. The green and red lamps are gas fired and manually controlled, and look much like railway signals. Unfortunately, the control mechanism fails and the lights blow up, killing the policeman controlling them and causing a passing platoon of cavalry to stampede. For some strange reason it then proved difficult to find anyone to man them.

1872 The first clampdown on drink-drivers. The Licensing Act 1872 makes it an offence to be drunk in charge of carriages, horses, cattle or steam engines. The penalty is a fine not exceeding 40s, or imprisonment for one month. Forty shillings equates to around £153 today, quite a modest punishment for drunken driving.

1878 Slightly better news for road users. The Highways and Locomotives (Amendment) Act 1878 relaxes the red flag law. The flag is made optional, subject to local regulations, and the walking distance is reduced to a more manageable 20yd in front. However, this did little to help the motorist, as there were in fact no cars as such.

A congested London in 1880.

The Wanderer caravan of 1885.

London steam tram of 1885.

Magnus Volk's dogcart.

1888 Benz.

1879 Mosley Street in Newcastle upon Tyne becomes the first street in the world to be lit by electricity. It is lit by Joseph Swan's incandescent lamps.

1880 As the 1880 photograph of London Bridge shows (see p.17), traffic in London is chaos even before the motor car came along to add to the problems. Forget driving on the left or right.

1885 The first leisure-touring caravan, the Wanderer, is built by Bristol Wagon Works for Dr William Gordon Staples. Horse-drawn, it took its first tour from Twyford to Inverness. Caravanning had begun, although many motorists on holiday roads would come to wish it hadn't.
■ Also in 1885 the first steam tram in the UK appears in London. It was not a great success as the noise is said to frighten passengers, and before long electric trams take over. However, steam trains had been running on the Metropolitan Line on the Underground for twenty-two years already without excessively frightening passengers.

1887 The first practical electric carriage, a three-wheeled 'dogcart', is built by Magnus Volk of Brighton. Volk had previously built, in 1883, the world's first electric railway along Brighton's seafront. Known as the Volk Electric Railway (VER) it still runs today. In 1896 he also built the Brighton & Rottingdean Seashore Electric Railway, also known as the 'Daddy Longlegs', an off-shore railway with the carriage raised up on 23ft legs, which lasted until 1901.

1888 John Boyd Dunlop 'invents' the pneumatic tyre independently of the earlier work of R.W. Thomson forty-three years earlier, and it is Dunlop's name which will forever be linked with the pneumatic tyre. The Dunlop Pneumatic Tyre Company Ltd is founded the following year. The Dunlop brand name still exists, but following a takeover by BTR in 1985 the company was split up and sold to different parties.

1888 There is disagreement about which was the very first motor car on British roads. Some sources say it was the 1888 Benz (bottom-left image), which now resides in the Science Museum in London. There are competing claims, however (see 1894 and 1895), although how a car can remain on the road unknown for six years does baffle me slightly.

The Pioneering Years

The first few years of the British motor industry saw many start-ups, but just six of these are even vaguely familiar names today: Lanchester (1895), Daimler (1896), Humber (1896), Wolseley (1896), Riley (1898) and Sunbeam (1899). Most of the others were small concerns which lasted maybe ten years at most and then disappeared forever. An important factor was that it was in these very early years that the overall nature of what a car should be like was evolving rapidly. None of the twenty-two 'losses' during the last decade of the nineteenth century are names which are generally known today. Overall there were twenty-one new businesses setting up and twenty-two closing down.

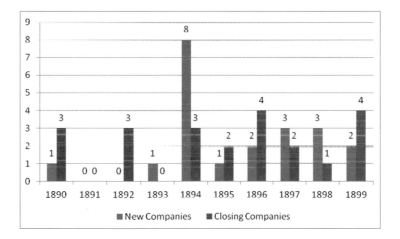

MILESTONES OVER THE AGES

Milestones are the oldest form of 'street furniture' and before the motor car they served an important function, telling the traveller how far he had to go until the next town. With few petrol stations in the early days of motoring, this information could help the motorist avoid running out of fuel.

The Romans first introduced milestones in Britain by measuring distances along their roads, marking every thousandth double-step with a large cylindrical stone – over 100 of these still survive today. The Latin for thousand is *mille*, from which the word mile is derived. The Roman *mille* was actually 1,618yd, rather than the 1,760yd we are used to. In the late eighteenth and nineteenth centuries the term 'long mile' was commonly used for 1,760yd, reflecting the historical differences between the two distances.

Following the departure of the Romans, roads developed much more to meet local needs. In 1555 an Act of Parliament required local parishes to take responsibility for the upkeep of their roads and install boundary markers, and in 1697 further legislation required guideposts at major junctions and in isolated places like moorland where traveller safety could critically depend upon distances.

The Turnpike Acts between 1706 and the 1840s created turnpike trusts to look after specific stretches of road, and from 1767 milestones became compulsory on all turnpikes. At the height of the turnpike era there were over 20,000 miles of road with milestones, most of which we still see today. When we see a milestone showing a distance to London, that distance always refers to the same reference point, which is the Eleanor Cross outside Charing Cross Station.

Ironically, it was the motor car which at first made milestones redundant, but which also later made them vital for different reasons. From the 1840s rail travel overtook road travel for long journeys, as it was quicker, safer and a lot more comfortable than horse-drawn coaches. Then with the advent of the motor car the importance of milestones waned further. Many were removed when roads were improved and many were taken away during the Second World War to baffle potential German invaders. Of the 20,000 or so which once existed, about 9,000 still survive.

However, the truth is that there are now very many more 'milestones', or at least distance marker posts, than there have ever been in the past, due to the advent of the motorway, which gave rise to a new need for motorists to understand their location. With limited access points and carriageways separated by a central reservation it is vital that emergency services know exactly where an accident is and which lane it is on. Similarly, maintenance workers need reference points, which in the old days might have been pubs or churches, but motorways are relatively featureless in that respect.

On motorways now there are two different 'milestones' or 'waymarkers'. Firstly, there are the distance marker posts, which are placed at 100m intervals. The posts give the distance in kilometres to a defined reference point for that road. Secondly, there are the larger driver location signs, which are generally placed every 500m and give the road name and the carriageway (generally 'A' is the carriageway going away from London and 'B' is the one going towards the capital).

Currently there are around 16,000 driver location signs and over 80,000 distance marker posts on British motorways. So, 'milestones' are actually more common than they ever have been and serve as a vital, if different, role from those of the turnpike days.

1894 Benz Velo.

1895 Panhard.

1891 Mr F.R. Simms acquires the Daimler rights in the UK, but with the intention of using their engines to power motor launches not motor cars. Simms's name will crop up quite a lot in the history of British motoring, although few people today recognise his name or the contribution he made.

1894 A second competing claim to be the first motor car on British roads is a 2hp Benz Velo imported by a Mr Henry Hewetson at a cost of £80, equivalent to £8,000 in today's money.

1895 The third competing claim to be the first car is a Daimler-powered Panhard et Levassor, brought over to the UK by F.R. Simms and Evelyn Ellis in 1895. They complete the long journey from Southampton to Malvern without incident, making this certainly the first long-distance British car journey.

■ *Autocar* magazine is founded, making it the oldest motoring magazine in the world. In 1895, however, its readership was somewhat limited, as car ownership could almost be counted on one hand.

■ Sir David Salomans organises Britain's first exhibition of motor vehicles in the open air in Tunbridge Wells. It was a somewhat modest show, featuring just five motor vehicles, including a steam tractor and a petrol-driven horse-drawn fire pump. There were two Panhard–Levassor engined vehicles and one De Dion tricycle. A few hundred people attended.

■ Later the same year the first indoor exhibition of cars takes place at the Stanley Cycle Show held in the Agricultural Hall, Islington. However, the motor car section only features two actual cars and two motor tricycles.

■ The Lanchester Brothers build the first 'all-British' four-wheel petrol-engined car, which appears on public roads the following year. Although it is labelled as all-British, it does in fact contain a few French and German components.

■ The 1895 Arrol Johnston, made in Glasgow, has an equal claim to be the first all-British car. Interestingly, Arrol Johnston continued production until 1928, after which no cars were built in Scotland until the Hillman Imp assembly lines were installed at Linwood near Glasgow in 1963.

■ There is disagreement over the first speeding ticket to be issued. It is reported that a Mr J.A. Koosen of Southsea is fined 1s in 1895 for driving at the reckless speed of 6mph. The court also levies costs of 15s 7d, a grand total of 83p, equivalent to £80 in today's money. However, there is a competing claim from 1896, as you shall discover further along in this timeline.

■ By the end of the year there are around fifteen cars on British roads.

1895 LANCHESTER

The 1895 Lanchester was the first really British four-wheeled, petrol-engined vehicle, although it had some foreign components. Work started in 1895 although it was not ready for sale until 1896. Unlike most of its contemporaries it was designed from the outset as a 'car' rather than a motorised horseless carriage. Initially it was powered by a single cylinder, 1,306cc engine, with the piston having two connecting rods to separate crankshafts rotating in opposite directions to give smoothness. These cars had tiller steering, worm final drive and epicyclic gearboxes.

1896 The first motor insurance policies appear, although it will not be compulsory to have insurance for many years and policies specifically exclude any damage caused by frightened horses. However, the risk of crashing into another car is somewhat remote. Indeed, even seeing another car is rare enough in 1896.

■ The Daimler Motor Company Ltd is founded and begins by selling imported Panhard and Peugeot cars.

■ The first British-built Daimler appears, although like the 1888 Benz it looked more like a carriage than a car. None will be sold until next year though.

■ The world's first electric starter motor is fitted to a motor car in Britain by Mr H.J. Dowsing, an electrical engineer. He installs his starter on an Arnold motor car – an adaptation of the Benz Velo – in East Peckham, Kent.

■ Herbert Austin, then running the the Wolseley Sheep Shearing Machine Company Ltd, builds the very first 'Wolseley' car. Working in his own time he builds his own version of the Léon Bollée that he had seen in Paris, known as the Wolseley Tricar. The following year he builds his second car, the Wolseley Autocar No. 1, a three-wheeler with one wheel at the front and two independently suspended rear wheels. The engine is a 2hp flat twin mid-mounted unit. However, although offered for sale at £110, it is not successful and none are sold, potential customers preferring a four-seat layout. His third effort, the four-wheeled Voiturette, has more success and did sell.

■ This is not a good year for Walter Arnold of East Peckham, Kent. He becomes another claimant to be the first person successfully charged with speeding, by driving at 8mph in a town where the limit was 2mph. He is fined 1s (£4.75p today) plus costs. Arnold had been pursued by a policeman on a bicycle, but there is no record of how the alleged speed was estimated – maybe it was the number of

1896 Wolseley Voiturette.

pedal turns per second. There is a competing claim for the first speeding fine (see 1895). This is East Peckham's second motoring 'first' in a year.

■ It is an even worse year for Bridget Driscoll, who becomes the victim of the first fatal car accident in Britain. Driscoll, aged 44, is knocked down and killed on her way to Crystal Palace. The car which knocks her down was travelling at only 4mph, but it is reported that Driscoll seemed bewildered and hesitated in front of the car; it is possible she'd never seen a car before and didn't know what it was. The coroner says he hopes it will be the last fatal accident on the roads of Britain. Some hope.

■ There is better news for the early motorists. The Locomotive and Highways Act 1896 sees the first improvements in motoring laws and was intended to encourage motor vehicles. Vehicles under 3 tons are to be exempt from the requirements of the 1878 Act, removing the need for a red flag, and the speed limit is raised to a heady 14mph.

■ The 1896 Act also makes lights and an audible warning, a horn or a bell, compulsory on all vehicles, in the interests of safety.

■ From 1896 all vehicles have to be registered by the County or County Borough Council. Heavy vehicles also have to be licensed.

■ Further regulations following on from the 1896 Act provide for a speed limit of 12mph, keeping to the left when passing oncoming traffic (cars, carriages, horses and cattle) and overtaking on the right-hand side. The regulations also include the requirement to stop upon request by a police constable or a person 'in charge of a restive horse'.

■ The relaxations introduced by the 1896 Act are celebrated by an informal drive from London to Brighton, organised by the British Motor Car Club. Fifty-eight cars enter, thirty-five successfully depart from London, and twenty-five make it safely to Brighton. The London to Brighton run has been repeated annually every November since, and the 'success' rate is now much higher!

1897 Richard Stephens, a mining engineer from South Wales, had seen the developments in motive power and in 1897 he produces his first car, which is made entirely by him, so can claim to be one of the first fully British cars. He goes on to produce twelve vehicles, including four- and six-seat cars and nine-seat buses, and so can also lay claim to being one of the very first serial production car companies.

■ Daimler sell their first domestically produced car, fitted with a Panhard engine. Later the same year they sell the first Coventry Daimler-engined vehicle and by

1897 DAIMLER 4HP
In 1897 Daimler start producing their first British Daimler cars, initially with Panhard engines. However, later that year the very first fully British 'Coventry' Daimler was manufactured, powered by a twin cylinder, 4hp engine with hot bulb ignition. Its top speed was 24mph and the price was £375.

mid-year are producing three of their own cars each week, as well as producing Léon Bollée cars under licence. They may claim to be the first serious serial car producer in Britain, turning out eighty-nine cars in the first eight months. The British motor industry is born.

■ A British-built Daimler is driven from John o'Groats to Land's End by Henry Sturmey, a journalist with *Autocar* magazine, demonstrating the feasibility of taking long motor car journeys.

■ The Automobile Club of Great Britain and Ireland is founded by F.R. Simms.

■ The first Blackwall Tunnel, the current westbound bore, opens to traffic.

■ London's first motor cabs are introduced in 1897 and are electrically powered. They are called Berseys after Walter C. Bersey, the manager of the London Electrical Cab Company who designed them, but are nicknamed 'Hummingbirds' from the sound that they make. Twenty-five are introduced in August 1897 and by 1898 a further fifty of them will be at work. Unfortunately, they prove costly and unreliable and there are a number of accidents, including one fatality. Public confidence in them evaporates and they are withdrawn by 1900.

1898 In what is believed to be the first death of a car driver resulting from an accident, Henry Lindfield of Brighton crashes and overturns his electrical carriage and has to have a leg amputated. He dies of shock the following day. *Autocar* blames the crash on 'excessive speed'.

■ Having been asked to improve S.F. Edge's Panhard, Montagu Napier builds his first engine, an 8hp vertical twin with electric ignition and installs it in Edge's vehicle. This will lead to full-scale car production in 1900.

■ The first Humber appears – a three-wheeler – and they enter serial production. Having shown the first models at the Stanley Cycle Show in 1896 they can also lay claim, along with Coventry Daimler, to be the start of the British motor industry. Humber would not make a four-wheel car until 1901.

1898 HUMBER SOCIABLE

Humber's first car, the Sociable. appears in 1898. A three-wheeler, it had seats side by side in a body mounted on C-springs. The single-cylinder engine was rated at 2.5hp and ran at a maximum of 750rpm. It had three speeds, an enclosed crankcase and the cylinder was placed horizontally and was air-cooled. The engine was manufactured for Humber by Accles-Turrell in Perry Bar, Birmingham. Having shown the first models at the Stanley Cycle Show in 1896 they can also lay claim, along with Coventry Daimler, to be the start of the British motor industry.

■Percy Riley builds his first car at the age of 16 secretly, as his father did not approve. Riley's car features the world's first mechanically operated inlet valves, previous engines all relying on suction from the piston to open the valve. His invention will prevent Benz from collecting royalties in Britain on 'their' invention of the mechanical valve, as the British courts determined that subsequent British cars using the system were based on Riley's earlier invention.

1899 This year sees the first accident where a driver or passenger is killed at the scene. The rear wheel of a 6hp Daimler collapses and Edwin Sewell and Major James Richer are thrown from their car. Sewell dies from his injuries at the scene at Grove Hill, Harrow. Sewell had been demonstrating the car to Major Richer, department head at the Army & Navy Stores, with a view to a possible purchase by the company. The major dies four days later without regaining consciousness. There is no record as to whether a sale subsequently took place, but it seems doubtful.
■Coventry Daimler release their first four-cylinder car, the previous original cars having been 1,526cc 'twins'.

1899 DAIMLER 12HP

The 12hp Daimler, first launched in 1899, was much more sophisticated than their previous models. It had a four-cylinder, 3,054cc engine delivering 12bhp, which could propel the car to 25mph. The inlet valves were still the antiquated automatic atmospheric type, and the suspension was still simple beam axles at the front and rear, but it looked much more like the sort of car we have come to know. It was fitted with pneumatic front tyres but solid rear ones. A 12hp Daimler holds the distinction of being the first car ever driven into the precincts of the Houses of Parliament.

■F.R. Simms (yes, him again!) builds the world's first petrol-driven armed vehicle, the Motor Scout, which consists of a Maxim machine gun mounted at the front of a De Dion-Bouton quadricycle. I suspect its main impact would be to scare the enemy rather than to actually shoot at him.

■Percy Riley offers two cars for sale, both called Royal Rileys, though they are little more than motorised tricycles, one with an extra wheel. They are, however, the world's first cars with wire wheels.

■By the end of the nineteenth century there are around 5,000 cars on the roads of Britain and there have already been mutterings about whether the roads could cope with any more traffic.

F.R. Simms' Motor Scout.

1899 ROYAL RILEY TRICAR

The Riley Cycle Co Ltd had been formed in 1896 through the merger of some local businesses in Coventry. Between 1896 and 1899 Percy Riley, one of the owner's sons, had built a car of his own, and although it never went into production it was the first car ever to use mechanically operated inlet valves, all previous cars using simple atmospheric valves. In 1899 the company offered two cars – a tricycle and a quadricycle – and both were referred to as 'Royal Rileys', although it is doubtful Queen Victoria ever graced one.

Motoring Becomes Established, for the Rich at Least!

The first decade of the twentieth century saw the largest ever number of new car companies start up in Britain, a total of ninety-seven being formed. However, it also saw many closures of businesses which proved not to be viable, with fifty-one closing. In the early days of any industry there are bound to be many unsuccessful start-ups, but the net increase of forty-six remains the largest ever seen for a ten-year period.

A number of more familiar names made their first appearance: Vauxhall (1903), Talbot (1903), Standard (1903), Rover (1904), Rolls–Royce (1904), Singer (1905), Lagonda (1906), Austin (1906), Jowett (1906), and Hillman (1907). A number of makes less familiar today, but important in their time, also appeared: Napier (1900), Albion (1900), Belsize (1901), Lea Francis (1903), Crossley (1904), and BSA (1907). The Maudsley appeared in 1902, as did the Siddeley, which would later evolve into the better known Armstrong Siddeley.

The decade was also not without some more amusing names. The Attila appeared in 1903, only to disappear again in 1906. Maybe the name did not appeal! The Napoleon made its appearance in 1903, and the quaintly named One of the Best saw the light of day in 1910. None of these lasted long. I wonder why?

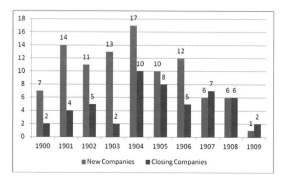

THE HISTORY OF ROAD SURFACES

Although maybe not the sexiest subject in the world, road surfaces matter to all of us and the history of road surfaces is actually quite interesting. A paved road surface provides the means for vehicles to move along without, rather importantly, sinking into the ground. How this is achieved has changed several times in the past. In terms of road history there have been six distinct eras:

Pre-Roman before 43 AD: Before the Romans arrived in Britain in 43 AD there was really very little need for roads. People didn't move far and what vehicle traffic there was consisted of just small, primitive carts. Roads, such as they were, were simple cleared tracks of earth and grass, sometimes used for the movement of cattle and sheep.

The Roman era 43 AD to 410 AD: When the Romans arrived they needed to move troops around the country quickly and efficiently, so substantial roads were built for the purpose, some of which survive today under modern roads. Roman construction was extremely expensive in terms of people's time but not cost, as they used slaves. It has been estimated that the cost today of building a Roman road would be around £1.5 million per kilometre – and that's just one lane's width. The Roman roads were over-engineered and could be nearly 1m thick. Figure 1 shows the structure of the typical British Roman road: 125mm of rubble was overlain by 400mm of course, lean mix concrete, and on top of that was 250mm of fine grain concrete, topped off by 100mm-thick paving slabs. Quite a pavement! Some Roman roads built on this principle, like the Appian Way, survive intact to this day.

The Dark Ages 410 to 1707: After the Romans left around 410 AD, British roads entered a sort of 'Dark Ages' up until the first Turnpike Acts in 1707. Many of the Roman roads survived fairly well, but other roads still depended upon local communities to repair what roads there were and in whatever way they could, which was usually next to nothing. In some areas the local landowners helped to keep the roads passable, but generally roads were unkempt muddy tracks which could become totally impassable in bad weather.

The early turnpikes 1707 to 1780s: The increasing amount of coach travel on the roads during the late eighteenth century led to them getting even worse. What had been really bad muddy tracks turned into terrible and dangerous muddy tracks. Something had to be done. The first Turnpike Acts in 1707 attempted to assign responsibility for road maintenance to local people and landowners and create Turnpike Trusts for this purpose. Up until the 1780s the success of the legislation was limited, partly because people just did not know how to improve their roads.

The scientific approach 1780s to 1901: In the 1780s two 'big names' appeared on the road front: Thomas Telford (born 1757) and John Loudon Macadam (born 1756). Both Scots, they came from very different backgrounds; Telford was born into poverty and became an orphan at an early age and Macadam was rich and from a titled family, but they both achieved greatness from their 'scientific' approach to road design. Their approaches were quite different. Telford's design, as shown in figure 2, relied, like the Romans, on a layer of large stones as a base, but did not include the heavy stone paving at the top. Macadam, on the other hand, did away with the need for any large stone layer and instead promoted a graded aggregate system, as shown in the figure 3. Telford's roads were expensive but long lasting; indeed, much of the old A5 Holyhead road is still based on Telford's original pavement. Macadam's roads were much cheaper but had a shorter design life. In the end both were actively used up until the late nineteenth century. It is interesting to reflect that both Telford's and Macadam's pavement designs were only about one third the thickness of the Romans' solution.

Tarmac and concrete 1901 to present: Ultimately Macadam's principles won the day. His graded layer approach, without any large stone layer, would become dominant. However, the growth of the motor car presented new problems not experienced in the days of horse transport. At speed, cars generated low pressure underneath, which tended to suck up dust from the road. Not only was this a handicap in terms of dust clouds, but the very dust itself had been intended to form a natural binding agent. The idea of adding a binding agent to hold the top layer together emerged in 1901, with the use of either sprayed tar or the application of a top layer of small stones mixed with tar, or, in exceptional cases, the use of natural Trinidad asphalt. In honour of Macadam's achievements the new paving material has become generally known as 'tarmac'.

From around the 1920s–30s concrete also started to emerge as a viable road structure. It became very popular in Germany and formed the basis of the autobahn system. It was not without problems, however, and never became popular with the British motoring public. Concrete roads were noisy and tended to develop cracks, as they were not flexible. Also, early concrete roads had been placed directly over a compacted soil base and would sometimes develop what was known as a 'pumping action', whereby slight up and down movements of the non-permeable road surface could, in wet conditions, actually erode the earth underneath. Although now remedied through incorporating a permeable gravel layer below, concrete roads have never gained much popularity in Britain. Looking to the future it's likely that Macadam's basic principles will still rule the day, whilst new and improved materials will continue to make our roads even safer and long lasting. Of particular significance is the emergence over the last few year of 'quiet' tarmac surfaces, which greatly reduce noise from traffic, especially in urban areas.

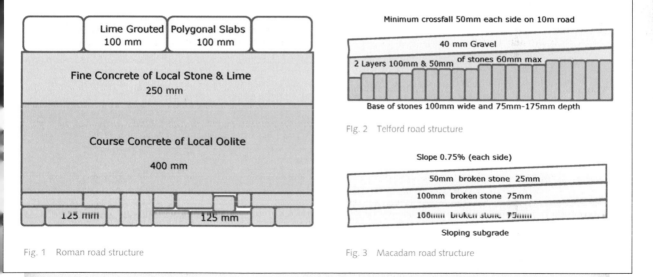

Fig. 1   Roman road structure

Fig. 2   Telford road structure

Fig. 3   Macadam road structure

1900 NAPIER

Montague Napier improved the design of a Panhard for S.F. Edge, but decided he wasn't happy with the design and could do better. In 1900 he built his first cars for sale, a batch of six, comprising three two-cylinder, 8hp, 2,436cc vehicles and three four-cylinder, 12hp and 4,872cc. The power output of the larger engine was a respectable 149bhp, giving a 0–60 time of 21.4 seconds. Napiers were always to be expensive cars, with the first model costing £500, which equates to £44,500 today. All Napiers were painted green, which is how British racing green came about.

1900 The Thousand Mile Trial is organised by the Automobile Club of Great Britain and Ireland in order to demonstrate the reliability and efficiency of the motor vehicle.

■The very first driving lessons in Great Britain are given by Mr Hankinson of the Motor Carriage Supply Company of London, but who the pupil was is not recorded, nor is the charge.

■After making his very first car in his spare time, and in secret, at the tender age of 16, Percy Riley makes his first car for sale – a three-wheeler Riley model.

■Montague Napier builds his first cars for sale – a batch of six, three with two cylinders (8hp) and three with four cylinders (12hp).

■Vera Hedges Butler becomes the first British person to pass her driving test. But she had to travel to France to take the test, since driver testing would not be introduced in the UK for another thirty years. Why she felt she needed to take any test at all remains a mystery. Maybe she just fancied a trip to France.

1901 The first speedometers become available on British cars as an optional extra.

■The first self-proclaimed 'driving school' is set up: the Liver Motor Car Depot and School of Automobilism in Birkenhead. The chief instructor is Archibald Frost.

■Lanchester start production of cars for sale to the public.

■Sunbeam, which had existed since 1888 making bicycles and then motorcycles and had made experimental cars since 1899, start production of cars for sale with the Sunbeam Mabley.

■Wolseley starts selling cars to the public and under Herbert Austin it will become, by 1906, Britain's biggest car manufacturer, selling 1,500 cars over five years.

■The first motorised hackney carriages appear in London.

1901 LANCHESTER 12HP

Lanchester started production of cars for sale to the public properly in 1901. The first was the 12hp powered by a 4,033cc twin-cylinder, horizontal air-cooled engine, retaining the earlier twin crankshaft design, and steering was by a side lever rather than a wheel. The gearbox was of epicyclic design. Lanchesters would always be expensive and rather quirky cars, intended to last 'forever'.

1901 SUNBEAM MABLEY

The first Sunbeam to enter series production, the Mabley, was of unconventional design, having its wheels set in a diamond formation, intended to reduce the risk of skidding. It was powered by a single cylinder, 2.75hp De Dion engine with an unusual cooling arrangement. The cylinder head was water cooled, whereas the block was air cooled. Drive was by belt from a two-speed gearbox. The driver sat at the back, steering by means of a tiller. When it first went on sale the Mabley cost £130 (£11,600 in today's money) and around 130 were made.

■Britain's first multi-storey car park is opened by the City & Suburban Electric Carriage Co. at 6 Denman Street, just off Piccadilly Circus, for the benefit of the owners of vehicles supplied by the company. The garage has seven floors and is equipped with an electric elevator capable of raising a 3-ton lorry to the top storey. With a total floor space of 19,000sq.ft, it is claimed as the largest garage in the world at that time.

■A Lloyds underwriter issues the first proper and comprehensive accident claim motor insurance policy. Finally the time has come when a collision between two cars is considered a possibility.

1902 The world's first disc brakes, an invention made by Frederick Lanchester, appear on a Lanchester 12hp car. However, the limitations of metallurgy at the time, and the poor state of the roads, which create a lot of grit on the discs, means that the discs wear out very quickly. Lanchester shelves the technology and it wouldn't reappear on a production car for another fifty years.

■The Society of Motor Manufacturers and Traders is formed by F.R. Simms (yes, him, yet again), who has been such a leading light in the early history of British motoring.

■The 8th Earl De La Ware, working in conjunction with the Automobile Club of Great Britain and Ireland, subsequently the Royal Automobile Club, organises the

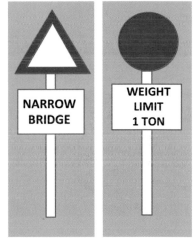

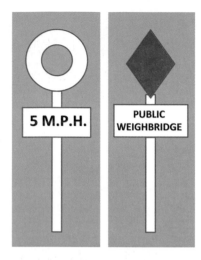

Vauxhall's first car, built in 1903.

first automobile racing on British soil at Bexhill-on-Sea. Such is the occasion that thousands flock to the town to witness the unique spectacle. The race is not on the road, however, but on the sand, as road racing is illegal in England.

1903 There are now around 17,000 motor vehicles registered in Great Britain.
■The government is clearly becoming concerned about the 'large' number of cars on the road and the lack of regulation, which leads to the Motor Car Act 1903. The Act introduces measures to help identify vehicles and drivers in the event of offences committed on the road. All drivers are to be licensed annually and all vehicles are to be registered and display registration marks. The vehicle registration fee is to be 20s and the driver's licence fee 5s.
■The Motor Car Act also raises the speed limit to 20mph, with Local Government Boards able to impose tighter limits of 10mph in more urban areas.
■The Motor Car Act creates four national road signs: a red warning triangle, a white speed limit ring, a diamond-shaped notice for information such as height restrictions, and a red 'prohibition' disc.
■The first motor race in Great Britain, the Gordon Bennett Cup, is held in Ireland (then part of Great Britain). Road racing is legal in Ireland but not in England, Scotland or Wales.
■The registration A1 is issued in London, although it was not actually the first registration in the country. The 'A' denotes a London registration, letters being linked to geography, as they are again today.
■Vauxhall build their first car, a 5hp model with tiller steering and two forward but no reverse gears. This quickly leads to an improved design.
■The first bus service to travel outside of a town is started in Cornwall, running a scheduled service from Helston to Lizard village. This same service still runs today, making it the country's oldest bus route.
■Napier announces the first six-cylinder British car for sale in 1904, the 4.9-litre 18hp. Within five years there would be no less than sixty-two manufacturers of six-cylinder cars in Britain alone.
■The Standard Motor Company builds its first cars: the single-cylinder 1-litre 6hp Motor Victoria with three-speed gearbox and shaft drive to the rear wheels. Between then and the end of 1904 they will be producing a car every three weeks.
■Lea Francis enter car production with a three-cylinder 3.5-litre 15hp model.
■The Society of Motor Manufacturers and traders (SMMT) hosts Britain's first motor show at Crystal Palace, with F.R. Simms at the helm (yes, he doesn't go away!).

1903 HUMBER 8HP HUMBERETTE

The Humberette is generally recognised as Britain's first popular light car. It was powered by a water-cooled, front-mounted, single-cylinder engine of 611cc, developing 5bhp, which was sufficient to give a top speed of 25mph. The engine drove the live rear axle via a propshaft, which was still quite a novelty in 1903 when most cars had chain drive. Suspension was by semi-elliptic springs all round and braking by a pair of hand-operated contracting bands on the rear axle. The standard car cost 125 guineas, although a superior model including luxuries like doors could be bought for 15 guineas more!

■This year sees the first use of windscreens on cars. However, they are a mixed blessing because, being made of ordinary glass, they are very dangerous, break easily and can inflict serious injury.
■Humber launch the 8hp Humberette, perhaps the first popular light car in Britain.
■The first petrol-powered cab appears in London. It is a French-built Prunel. Early British makes included Rational, Simplex and Herald, but these only appear in small numbers.

1904 There is the very first mention in 1904 of a 'New Slough Road' consisting of four lanes to relieve the traffic congestion in the town centre, by then a major stop on the Great Western Railway. This would be the precursor of the Slough and Maidenhead bypass, which would eventually evolve into the M4 when this section was opened fifty-seven years later.
■Alldays & Onions launch their very successful 7hp model.
■Henry Royce builds his first motor car, and later the same year meets Hon. Charles Rolls, whose dealership in London sells quality cars. The company Rolls-Royce was, however, not created until 1906.
■Ford begins exporting cars to Britain. The first, their Model A, will never become very popular here and it will soon be replaced firstly by imported Model Ts, then domestically built Ts, which are to become a great success.

1904 Royce.

1904 ALLDAYS & ONIONS 7HP

Alldays & Onions started making cars as early as 1899, with a quadricycle powered by a single cylinder De Dion engine. In 1904 they launched the 7hp, which looked very modern, but it was still powered by a single-cylinder side-valve engine of just 926cc rated at 7hp. However, it became one of Britain's most successful small cars and it sold in considerable numbers until 1908.

1904 ROVER 8HP

The 8hp, Rover's first car, had an unusual design. Instead of a conventional chassis it had a 'backbone' formed by the engine crankcase, gearbox housing, prop shaft housing and rear axle. The backbone chassis had no suspension at the rear apart from that provided by the tyres, but the body was mounted on the rear axle by semi-elliptical springs. At the front the axle was suspended from the backbone by a transverse leaf spring. The engine was a single-cylinder 1,327cc unit. It had an unusual additional pedal which changed the valve operating cam to provide engine braking. The basic model cost £200.

1904 WOLSELEY 12HP HORIZONTAL TWIN

The 12hp Wolseley, designed by Herbert Austin, featured a 2.6-litre twin-cylinder engine, forward mounted and set between the bonnet sides which were the cooling elements for the radiator. The engine featured detachable cylinder heads containing the vertical valves (atmospheric inlets) and cast-iron cylinder liners fitting into the aluminium crank chamber and water jacket. Drive was through a cone clutch and inverted tooth Renold silent chain to a three-speed gearbox with final drive by side chains. Production continued until late 1905.

1904 Riley Forecar.

■ Percy Riley is still offering cars which are little more than motorised tricycles, including the Forecar, which would remain in production for another two years.

■ Rover starts making cars, with its 8hp model.

■ The 12hp Wolseley is introduced.

■ There are now 28,842 vehicles on the roads of Great Britain, an increase of 70 per cent over the previous year. Can the roads take any more?

1905 Herbert Austin leaves Wolseley to form his own company at Longbridge, which will eventually grow into BMC and then British Leyland, absorbing Wolseley somewhere along the way. What a wise move!

■ Riley start to sell its Vee-Twin Tourer. Two years later they will concentrate solely on car production and stop making bicycles and motorcycles.

■ Although Singer had been producing motorised three wheelers since 1901, these were more like motorcycles than cars. Their first proper car appears in 1905, with a two-cylinder engine of 1,853cc or 2,471cc, which was a variant of a Lea Francis design.

■ The first Brighton Speed Trials are held on a ¼-mile stretch of Madeira Drive organised by the Brighton & Hove Motor Club. The speed trials continue to this day, making them

1905 RILEY 9HP V-TWIN

Although the Riley brothers had made their first three-wheeled tricar as early as 1900, they did not produce a four-wheeled vehicle until 1905. Rated at 9hp, it used a 1,034cc V-twin engine mounted amidships with the gearbox alongside and chain final drive. It sold for £168. From 1908 onwards a larger 2-litre version was offered with a more conventional layout and a rounded radiator. The 9hp V-twin would, in 1907, become the first car to have wire wheels as standard.

the world's longest-running motoring event, although some years have been skipped. The fastest time of the day at the first event was recorded by a 90hp Napier.

■The AA is set up to represent the interests of motorists finding themselves easy targets for the police. One early duty of the AA patrolmen is to warn members of police speed traps. This will result in a legal challenge in 1910.

■Britain's first transporter bridge, carrying vehicles on a suspended platform just above the water, is built between Runcorn and Widnes. It will be demolished in 1961 when a replacement bridge is built.

Brighton Speed Trials.

■Having been an importer of French cars since the company was set up in 1903, Talbot start selling cars assembled in Britain from French components in 1905. Domestically designed cars follow in 1906.

■The Automobile Club becomes the governing body for motor sport in Britain.

1906 Rolls-Royce launch the iconic Silver Ghost and gain the accolade of the 'best car in the world'; a title Rolls-Royce has keenly hung onto ever since.

■Britain exports just two cars a month to France but imports 400 French cars. The French have always been very patriotic about their car industry, and remain so to this day.

■Britain's second transporter bridge is built at Newport, but unlike the first at Runcorn this one still survives.

Runcorn transporter bridge.

■Austin starts producing cars for sale.

■Jowett produce their first car. However, as their workshop is busy with general engineering work, engine development and assembly of Scott motorcycles, it does not go into full production until 1910, after 25,000 miles of testing. It has a flat twin 816cc engine of 6.4hp, a three-speed gearbox and tiller steering. The flat engine configuration will remain a defining feature of Jowett cars, and Bradford Jowett vans, until they cease trading in 1955.

1906 ROLLS-ROYCE SILVER GHOST

The Silver Ghost really made Rolls-Royce's reputation. Compared to contemporary cars it was silent, smooth, ultra reliable and supremely elegant. With a 7,036cc side-valve straight six, it was not fast, as in many cases it was called upon to haul around heavy coach-built bodies weighing up to 2.5 tons. The Silver Ghost was produced right up until 1926, mechanically the same but with increasingly modern coachwork.

1906 AUSTIN 25/30

The 25/30 and its sister the 15/20 were Herbert Austin's first cars after he had created the Austin Motor Company. Unlike most of his later cars, it was right at the upper end of the price scale. The £650 for a complete car equates to £57,420 today! The smaller engined 15/20 was cheaper at £500. Over a period of two years sixty-seven were made. The engine was a four-cylinder T-head of 5,182cc, giving the car a top speed of 44mph.

■Lagonda is founded by an American, Wilbur Gunn, and named after Lagonda Creek, the town of his birth. He launches his first car the following year, the 20hp six-cylinder Torpedo. In the early years Lagonda also makes a very advanced small car, the 11.1 with a 1-litre four-cylinder engine, which features an anti-roll bar, rivetted monocoque body and the first ever fly off hand brake.
■Steam trams are still widely used around Birmingham.

1907 King Edward VII awards the Automobile Club the 'Royal' accolade, and it becomes the RAC.
■60,000 cars are now registered in Great Britain.
■Brooklands opens as the world's first purpose-built race track. Racing on public roads is illegal, except on the Isle of Man, so the poodle-breeding jigsaw addict Hugh Fortescue Locke-King builds a track on his estate. Two thousand labourers clear 30 acres of woodland to make way for the track, parts of which still survive.
■A Rolls-Royce Silver Ghost completes a test of 15,000 miles duration under RAC supervision with just one enforced stop, underlining the quality of the Rolls-Royce product.
■AA Patrols begin, with the patrolmen, at first, on bicycles.

Brooklands race track.

38

■Meters are introduced to govern the fares charged by motorised hackney carriages in London. They are called 'taximeters', after their German inventor Baron von Thurn und Taxis. However, there is a competing explanation (and a better documented one) for the name 'taxi', which is that it was invented by Wilhelm Bruhn, not a baron, in 1891 and that the word comes from the German word *taxe*, meaning a charge or levy. Does it really matter? We still pay anyway.

1908 The 1908 Finance Act passes responsibility for collecting the revenue from Excise Licensing from the Commissioners for the Inland Revenue to County and County Borough Councils.
■The Act also announces a *3d* per gallon tax on petrol – the first duty on fuel – equivalent to just over £1 in today's money. Some things never change!
■The AA publishes its first members' handbook.
■Rolls-Royce open their factory in Derby where they remain to this day building aero engines. However, upon the car division being recently purchased by BMW, production of the Phantom and Ghost has moved to a dedicated factory in Goodwood, West Sussex.

1909 In her book *The Woman and the Car* Dorothy Levitt provides information and advice about motoring to society ladies, which includes a recommendation that all ladies should carry a small revolver.
■Britain's first roundabout is built in Letchworth, just five years after the world's first at Columbus Circle, New York. Originally called Sollershott Circus, traffic circulates in either direction, the discipline of the roundabout not emerging until the 1920s when 'keep left' signs were installed. The roundabout in Letchworth remains to this day, unchanged, apart from some enlargement.
■In the light of the poor state of most roads, the 1909 Development and Road Improvement Funds Act provides grants to local authorities for approved highway works.
■The Finance Act 1909–10 announces a vehicle tax based on the nominal horsepower of the vehicle, a system developed in conjunction with the RAC and which remains in place until 1949. The Act also states that all revenues will be used solely for road improvements. This pledge started to be relaxed in the 1930s, although the excise licence is still often called the road fund licence.
■Petrol tax announced under the Finance Act 1908 comes into force.

Britains first roundabout.

The First Signs of Creeping Regulation

The second decade of the twentieth century was interrupted by the First World War, during which the number of new car companies set up was drastically reduced. However, the total number of new car businesses over the whole decade was, at sixty-nine, the second largest ever seen, as was the net increase of thirty-four.

A few familiar names appeared: Morgan (1910), Morris (1913), Bentley (1919), Alvis (1919) and Armstrong Siddeley (1919). Other makes important in their day appeared, including GN (1910), Invicta (1913) and Guy (1919). The decade also saw two amusing new makes: Tiny (1912) and Utopian (1914). Neither lasted long; maybe one was too small and the other too perfect.

Amongst the thirty-five names which disappeared none is familiar today.

By 1919 the total number of British car manufacturers had reached 110.

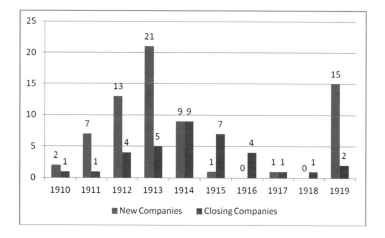

THE HISTORY OF SPEED LIMITS

1829: Perhaps the need for speed limits first became evident when Goldsworthy Gurney's steam carriages were attaining the dizzy speed of 20mph in London, scaring pedestrians and horses alike. Many of us must long for the days when 20mph was actually possible in London.

1861: The Locomotive Act 1861 limited the weight of steam engines to 12 tons and imposed a speed limit of 10mph.

1865: The Highways and Locomotives Act 1865 set a new speed limit of 4mph in the country and 2mph in towns for motorised vehicles. The Act also required the 'man with the red flag' who had to walk 60yd ahead of each vehicle with a red flag or lantern to enforce a walking pace and warn horse riders and horse-drawn traffic of the approach of a self-propelled machine. This rule would last into the early days of the motor car.

1878: The Highways and Locomotives (Amendment) Act 1878 relaxed the red flag law slightly. The flag was made optional subject to local regulations and the walking distance was reduced to a more manageable 20yd in front, but the speed limit remained.

1896: The Locomotive and Highways Act 1896 made motor vehicles under 3 tons exempt from the requirements of the 1878 Act, removing the need for a red flag and raising the speed limit to a heady 14mph.

1903: The Motor Car Act 1903 raised the speed limit to 20mph, with local government boards able to impose tighter limits of 10mph in more urban areas.

1930: A golden year for the motorist. All speed limits are abolished under the Road Traffic Act 1930, but 30mph limits are imposed on coaches, buses and most heavy goods vehicles.

1934: A general 30mph limit in built-up areas is introduced. The existence of street lights closer than 100yd apart without any displayed de-restriction sign on the lamp posts is taken as being a 30mph limit by default, as it still is.

1940: A 20mph limit for night-time driving in built-up areas is imposed to help reduce the terrible accident rate during the blackout.

1956: The Road Traffic Act 1956 makes the 30mph limit in built-up areas permanent.

1957: The maximum speed limit for goods vehicles is raised from 20mph to 30mph.

1965: A 70mph blanket speed limit is introduced as a four-month experiment, following the reported test drive of an AC Cobra at 150mph on the M1.

1965: A new 50mph limit is introduced on certain rural trunk roads.

1966: The speed limit for PSVs is raised from 40mph to 50mph.

1967: The national 70mph limit, introduced as an 'experiment' in 1965, is made permanent. It is not referred to as a '70mph' limit, but as 'the national limit', opening the door for future changes without major new legislation.

1967: A 30mph limit on motorways when the visibility is restricted by fog is introduced, to be indicated by flashing amber lights.

1973: As a result of the Arab-Israel War and fuel shortages a blanket 50mph limit is imposed.

1974: The temporary 50mph limit is lifted as the conflict ceases.

1977: A 30mph speed limiter is made a requirement for mopeds.

1978: The national speed limit on ordinary roads is set at 60mph, with the national limit remaining at 70mph on motorways and dual carriageways.

1984: The Road Traffic Regulations Act 1984 exempts emergency vehicles from speed limits when responding to emergency calls.

1991: New 20mph zones are introduced in residential areas and near schools.

1991: Speed limiters are required for buses and coaches, set at 65mph. For heavy goods vehicles the limiters are set at 56mph.

1995: Variable mandatory speed limits are introduced on the M25 replacing advisory speeds, controlled by the Motorway Incident Detection and Automatic Signalling (MIDAS) system.

1999: Local authorities are given the power to impose 20mph limits on any local road without requiring the approval of the Secretary of State.

2010: The Department of Transport proposes a limit of 65mph for all vehicles which can carry eight or more people.

1910 RAC-devised horsepower ratings, used for taxing cars, come into force. Charges are £2 10s for cars up to 6.5hp, rising to £42 for 60hp (equivalent to a massive £3,500 today!). The RAC horsepower rating is based on engine dimensions and has nothing to do with the power output like brake horsepower does.

■The Hon. Charles Rolls, partner with Henry Royce, is killed in a plane crash aged just 33. The company changes the colour of the car's badge from red to black as a sign of respect and mourning.

■The habit of AA patrolmen warning members about police speed traps is challenged in court. The AA then switch to a 'coded' signal, whereby the patrolman, who would normally salute a car carrying an AA badge, would omit the salute if a speed trap were ahead. Members are requested to 'challenge' any patrolman who does not salute, upon which the warning about the speed trap would be given; this cannot be challenged in court.

AA patrolman. (Courtesy of the Automobile Association)

■Motor 'houses', the forerunner of the humble garage, start to become popular on large country estates. Often the motor house would have living accommodation above for the chauffeur and/or mechanic.

■The same year, what is believed to be Britain's first 'car port' is built at Sutton Hoo to house the owner's Daimler.

Britain's first car port at Sutton Hoo.

1910 MORGAN

Having built a prototype for himself in 1909, Henry Frederick Stanley Morgan starts producing cars for sale in 1910. The first production Morgans are single seaters with tiller steering and either a single-cylinder 4hp engine or an 8hp V-twin. A feature was an extraordinarily good power to weight ratio of 90bhp per ton, making then as fast as any car on the road at the time. One thing which set Morgans apart from other cyclecars was its independent front suspension by a simple sliding-pillar design, a genuine revolution for solid-axle 1910, and one that would stay with Morgan up to today.

1910 GN

GN started producing lightweight cars in 1910 powered by V-twin JAP or Peugeot motorcycle engines, with belt drive to the rear wheel. Like Morgans they had very high power-to-weight ratios and would become fearsome competitors in hill-climb events. The first models weighed just 180kg (397lb) and were easily capable of 60mph, a good speed for 1910. The company had a relatively short life, however, ceasing trading in 1925, but around 200 were made.

An Argyll Flying 15 equipped with four-wheel breaking.

Rolls-Royces' Spirit of Ecstasy mascot.

■ Crossley, Arrol-Johnston and Argyll start to offer four-wheel braking, something which would remain quite a novelty for several years to come. There was a belief that brakes on front wheels would be dangerous and promote skids.
■ The first production Morgans appear.
■ The same year a rival cycle car appears in the form of the first GN.

1911 The Rolls-Royce mascot the Spirit of Ecstasy first appears. The world's most famous car mascot was the work of sculptor and illustrator Charles Sykes, who was commissioned to design the famous icon by Henry Royce. The model for the sculpture was Eleanor Thornton, who was a secretary at the car magazine where Sykes worked. Having been killed the year before, the Hon. Charles Rolls never saw the iconic mascot which would become so strongly associated with the marque and its quality.
■ Britain's third transporter bridge is built at Middlesbrough, and still survives together with the one at Newport.
■ The Ford Motor Company (England) Ltd is incorporated and Model T assembly begins at a converted tram works in Trafford Park, Manchester. The company initially employs sixty people.

1912 The first motor museum in Britain opens inside Waring & Gillow's department store on Oxford Street. The museum only lasted two years and many of the exhibits were subsequently dumped on waste ground near Charing Cross Station and simply left to rot away.
■ The Bentley brothers buy the London agency for the French DFP cars, a precursor to the Bentley car company.
■ Walter Owen (W.O.) Bentley competes in sporting events in a DFP.
■ Napier launch their 40/50hp.

1912 NAPIER 40/50
In 1912 Napier launch their advanced 40/50hp, with a 6,177cc all-alloy six-cylinder engine, with single overhead cam, seven bearings, dual plugs, coil ignition and dual magnetos. The 40/50 was an extremely expensive motor car and just 187 were built between 1912 and 1924. By 1919 the list price for a 40/50 chassis, with no bodywork, was £2,185 (equivalent to around £82,500 today), whereas the equivalent Rolls-Royce was just £1,575. Good coachwork could double the price. The photograph is from a contemporary sales brochure.

■The AA introduce roadside telephone boxes, most of which have now vanished, being made virtually redundant by the mobile phone.
■The AA also starts inspecting hotels and restaurants and rating them for their handbook.

1913 Work on classifying roads relating to quality and usage is started by the Government's Road Board. However, the work will be interrupted by the First World War and will not resume until 1919 under the new Ministry of Transport.
■The first roadside petrol pumps appear, starting with one in Shrewsbury. However, they would not appear in great numbers until 1920 when the AA set up a network of filling stations for members.
■William Morris launches his first car, the 10hp 2-seater Morris Oxford light car at a cost of £175 (£14,145 at today's prices). They are made in the former Oxford Military College at Cowley. From 1915 it will be followed by a smaller engined version called the Cowley, which will gain the nickname 'Bullnose' and will be an instant success.
■Ford make 6,000 Model Ts at Trafford Park this year, making it the biggest selling car at the time.
■Humber is now the second largest car maker, operating out of Coventry in a factory which still exists in spite of the city's destruction in the Second World War.
■William Rootes lays the foundations for the Rootes Group by setting up a car dealership in Hawkhurst, Kent.
■The very first car to bear the name Aston Martin appears in 1913. Lionel Martin and Robert Bamford found the Company in 1913 and produce their first car, which is a 1908 Isotta-Fraschini chassis fitted with a four-cylinder Coventry Simplex engine. They plan to go into full production from premises in Kensington in 1915, but the war will prevent their plans coming to fruition.

The first telephone boxes were introduced by the AA in 1912. (Courtesy of the Automobile Association)

MORRIS COWLEY 'BULLNOSE'
The Cowley 'Bullnose' was William Morris's second model and was a great success, even being called Britain's 'Model T Ford'. However, whereas Henry Ford insisted on making everything in-house, Morris bought in most components from external suppliers. It was a simple, robust design, with a 1,548cc side-valve four-cylinder engine, delivering a modest 26bhp at 2,800rpm. It was fairly light at 1,750lb and so could achieve a respectable 50mph. Eventually over 54,000 would be produced.

1914 The last horse bus ceases operating in London.

■ Britain's first moving assembly line is built by Ford at Trafford Park, making the Model T. The Ford factory would much later play a vital role in the Second World War by turning out over 30,000 Rolls-Royce Merlin engines. Ford could make the engines more accurately than Rolls-Royce, enabling part interchangeability.

■ Most car production facilities cease private car manufacture and are switched to wartime production.

1915 The Government introduces a 'temporary' 33.33 per cent import duty on luxury items, including cars, to help pay for the war.

■ The 'tank' is invented and many large, powerful luxury car chassis – in particular the Rolls-Royce Silver Ghost – are assembled as armoured cars, as they are capable of carrying the very heavy armour.

■ The first car with a dipstick to check oil level is launched – the 1915 Morris Cowley. Unlike many automotive inventions this one is still used, unchanged in nearly all cars today.

The Ford factory at Trafford Park.

ROLLS-ROYCE SILVER GHOST ARMOURED CAR

The Silver Ghost was so solidly made that it formed the basis for a successful armoured car in the First World War, with the Royal Naval Air Service raising the first armoured car squadrons in 1914. All available Silver Ghost chassis were requisitioned for conversion and six squadrons each of twelve cars were formed. The large, lowly stressed Rolls engine, turning out a modest 80bhp, was able to move the 4.7-ton vehicles at up to 45mph (72kph) and allowed a range of 150 miles (240km). Armament was a 0.303in Vickers machine gun.

1916 The London 'Safety First' Council is formed, later to become in 1941 Royal Society for the Prevention of Accidents (RoSPA).

1917 Because of the continuing war effort there is virtually no news on the private motor car front this year.

1918 The first painted road markings appear: the single solid white line to indicate 'no overtaking'.

■Wolseley begin a joint venture in Tokyo with Ishikawajiama Ship Building and Engineering. The first Japanese-built Wolseley car rolls off the line in 1922. After the Second World War, the Japan venture will be reorganised, renaming itself Isuzu Motors in 1949. Today, Isuzu is part of General Motors.

1919 Mixed news for the motorist. The tax on petrol is abolished but higher rates of excise duty are introduced to maintain Government revenues.

■Seeing the need for reform, the Road Board is abolished and its functions transferred to the new Ministry of Transport.

■Work on classifying roads on the basis of quality and usage, started in 1913, is resumed under the new Ministry and is proposed as the basis for allocating funds for road maintenance. Roads will be classified as Class I, important routes connecting large population centres, and Class II, roads of lesser importance. Smaller roads would remain unclassified. The final list will be published in 1923.

■Bentley Motors Ltd is formed and their first design, the 3-litre, is a highly innovative vehicle. Although shown at the 1919 London Motor Show, with orders being taken by December for delivery in 1920, development takes longer than expected and cars are not delivered until 1921. Interestingly, the Bentley 3-litre is the first British car ever to be described in 'litres', which confuses people used to cars being described by nominal 'RAC horsepower'.

■By the first year after the war, 41 per cent of all cars registered in Great Britain are Fords, a dominance by one manufacturer which would never be seen again.

■The first British caravan for towing by car is produced, the 'Eccles', built by J.M. Riley. Caravanning quickly becomes popular and by 1925 the RAC has created a Caravan Department.

The Eccles caravan first appeared in 1919.

BENTLEY 3-LITRE
Bentley's first car would become a great success on the track and on the road. Between 1919 and 1929, when it was replaced by the 4.5-litre car, 1,622 were produced. It was powered by a straight four of 2,743cc with a single overhead camshaft and four valves and two spark plugs per cylinder. Although a heavy car at 4,000lb (1,800kg) the engine was powerful and strong. The car won the Le Mans 24 Hour Race in 1924 and 1927. Because of its size, weight and speed Ettore Bugatti called it 'the fastest lorry in the world'.

1919 GUY V8

Guy Motors Ltd had been formed in 1914 to manufacture lorries using a new lightweight technique of pressed steel frames. In 1919 they branched out into cars, deciding to focus on the luxury sector. Their first car was a 4-litre V8-engined vehicle, shown in the photograph, the first British V8 rated at 20hp. This car was also the first in the world to have a completely automatic chassis lubrication system. Every time the steering went to full right lock, a ratchet worked a pump which sent lubricating oil to all the key points on the chassis.

■The Alvis Car Company is formed, and develops its first car, the 10/30, which goes on sale the following year.

■In 1919 the company of Siddeley-Deasy, which had been making quality cars since 1912, is taken over by Armstrong Whitworth of Newcastle, and Armstrong Siddeley is formed as a subsidiary. The first Armstrong Siddeley is a massive 5-litre 30hp vehicle, setting the scene for what will become a luxury upmarket marque. The cost of the 30hp is around £1450, or nearly £76,000 in today's money. Smaller models will follow, but still very much at the luxury end of the market.

■The Metropolitan Police introduce Britain's first police cars. But rather than being used to catch offenders the sixteen vehicles are for the exclusive personal use of Assistant Commissioners and Superintendents.

■Guy Motors Ltd launches the first British V8-powered car.

The Beginning of Motoring for the Masses

The third decade of the twentieth century saw the first decline in the number of car companies – a net loss of eleven. Although sixty-three new businesses started, a record seventy-four closed down. This was mainly a reflection of many start-up businesses just not having the momentum, scale advantage or technological edge to survive in a market increasingly dominated by large manufacturers.

Four well-known makes came into being: Leyland (1920), later better known for trucks than cars; Aston Martin (1921); MG and Triumph (1923); and Frazer Nash (1924). However, several important companies disappeared: Leyland as a car maker (1923); Napier (1924); GN (1925); and BSA (1926).

The '20s also gave us some amusing companies: Gerald and Albert both appeared, albeit briefly, as car manufacturers.

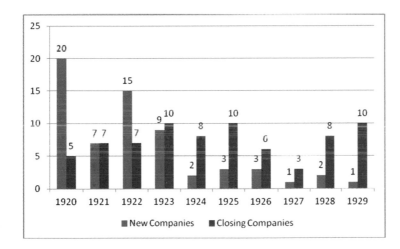

LONDON'S RINGWAYS

The M25 is the longest ring road in the world, and many people probably think it is a recent idea. In fact London has a long history of plans to relieve traffic pressure by constructing ring roads, most of which came to nothing. The first 'bypass' of London, the wide New Road connecting Paddington to Islington (the road we now know as Marylebone Road), was started in 1756 so that through traffic could avoid the congested city centre. When it was built it marked the very edge of the built-up area, but not for long! However, it does now mark the edge of the congestion zone. After that very little happened until the twentieth century.

The ensuing milestone was the Royal Commission on London Traffic set up in 1903. The Board of Trade watered down the commission's recommendations considerably, but their report, the General Road Plan published in 1911, did propose 100 miles of new roads, including the North Circular and Eastern and Western Avenues. Due to the First World War work did not start immediately, but the roads had been completed by the mid-1930s, although not as the dual carriageways originally envisaged.

The next step forward was the Highway Development Survey of 1937. Engineer Sir Charles Bressey and architect Sir Edwin Lutyens carried out a major review of transport needs in a city that had grown rapidly with the development of the London Underground. Apart from the many recommendations about central London, perhaps the most significant were for north and south orbital roads, at a radius of about 20 miles from the city centre. Eventually only a short section of the North Orbital would be built, which exists to this day.

Once again war got in the way of major construction, but not in the way of planning. The key name in the next phases was Patrick Abercrombie, the professor of town planning at University College London. He produced two plans: the County of London Plan 1943 and the Greater London Plan 1944. The former focused on arterial roads in and out of central London, with three classes of road: Arterial Roads with no access to side streets and no direct frontages, Sub-Arterial Roads with service roads and limited access to side streets, and Local Roads. In addition, three major ring roads, A-Ring, B-Ring and C-Ring, were proposed. The A-Ring corresponded very much to the Inner Ring Road today, which largely defines the Congestion Zone; the C-Ring was effectively the North and South Circulars; and the B-Ring was halfway in between. For his Greater London Plan, Abercrombie proposed two further ring roads outside the C-Ring, called the D-Ring and the E-Ring, the latter being a revised version of the North and South Orbital Roads, sections of which would be built. The plan also proposed ten principal radial routes, mainly improvements of what already existed, like the A40, A4, A3 and so on.

Scarcely had the ink dried on Abercrombie's plan when the highway engineers of the 1950s began to realise his plans were at odds with astronomical forecasts for traffic growth. A major rethink was needed. Initially they proposed that the innermost ring, the A-Ring, would be built to full motorway standard and that major arterial roads, like the already planned M1, would go right to the centre of London and join it. In the end, of course, the staggering cost of building a full motorway right in the centre of London killed this plan.

Things went very quiet until the early 1960s, or so it seemed; in fact, the planners were working furiously in secret. The plans emerged in a bizarre way when Battersea Borough Council wanted to build a swimming bath, but try as they might they couldn't get planning permission. In the end the London County Council (LCC) had to 'come clean' about their ambitious plans, although Battersea Borough Council need not have worried too much because in 1965 the LCC was disbanded and replaced by the Greater London Council (GLC). As is human nature, the GLC planners and engineers wanted to stamp their own authority on the plans, so Abercrombie's 'Rings' were replaced by Ringway 1, Ringway 2, Ringway 3 and Ringway 4. Similarly, Abercrombie's 'Radial' roads were given new names so that, for example, 'Radial Route 7' became the 'M12'.

In 1966 the London Motorway Box, Ringway 1, went public and was revealed to the press, followed by the publishing of Ringway 2 in 1969. Interestingly all the London boroughs affected by these plans were supportive at first, but the plans would die as a result of the exorbitant costs, which central government refused to cover, and increasingly fierce public disapproval. By 1973, the ringways had effectively died, but also that year the Ministry of Transport started work on part of Ringway 3, which was to be called the M16. Construction took two years, but before it was completed things changed yet again! In 1974 the Ministry announced that the M16 would be merged with a new motorway, to be called the M25, which would also incorporate the southern and western sections of Ringway 4. The plan for a complete circular motorway removed the need for the most controversial part of the plan, Ringway 3. Shortly afterwards the government announced the complete cancellation of Ringway 2, on the grounds that the M25 made it and the other ringways unnecessary.

The original Abercrombie plan had identified the need for not only the M25, but also for three other inner ring roads built to motorway standard. In the end we got just the M25 and nothing at all to relieve the South Circular, still to this day a hotchpotch of old roads which exists more in the mind than in reality!

The map shows the ringways as planned and the parts which were built. Today, the M25 combines most of the southern section of Ringway 4 with the northern section of Ringway 3 (the dotted line shows roughly how they join). The north section of Ringway 2 is effectively the upgraded North Circular, whilst of the innermost Ringway 1 most was never built. There is, however, a ¾-mile section of the innermost ring connecting the Holland Park roundabout and the A40(M) Westway, which used to be called the M41 until 2000 when it was downgraded. Part of the eastern section was also constructed.

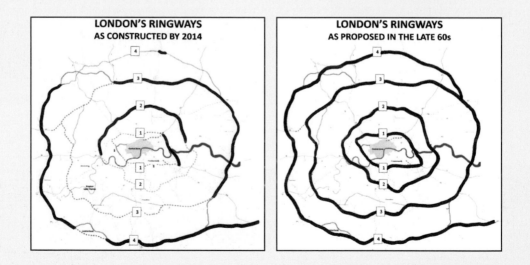

LONDON'S RINGWAYS
AS CONSTRUCTED BY 2014

LONDON'S RINGWAYS
AS PROPOSED IN THE LATE 60s

1920 Britain's first purpose-built 'drive in' petrol filling station opens in Aldermaston, Berkshire. It is operated by the AA and can only be used by AA members. The hose from the pump passes through the window of the wooden building – no health and safety worries in those days, then. The AA builds around ten of these, but today all the sites have completely vanished.

■The first London Motor Show takes place. The show occupies both Olympia and White City and includes 174 makes of car. Today the same motor show only displays cars from around fifty manufacturers.

■The Great West Road is opened as a new route out of London avoiding many villages and towns. It is the first new major route into and out of the capital built since the dawn of the motor car. Later, in 1925, it will become the country's first purpose-built dual carriageway.

Britain's first petrol station at Aldermaston.

■The Roads Act 1920 is the first Act which is aimed specifically at the motor car. Previous legislation had been aimed at all road vehicles and traffic in general.

■The Act requires councils to register all vehicles at the time of purchase and to allocate a separate number to each vehicle. It also requires the number to be displayed in an approved manner; registration plates have started.

■The Act introduces the concept of a General Licence, the forerunner to modern trade plates for manufacturers and traders. In addition, hackney carriages would now have to display a special sign showing how many passengers they can carry, just as they still do today.

The new Great West Road in 1920.

■The concept of a vehicle's 'keeper' replaces that of the vehicle's owner on the log book, with implications for the responsibility for law infringement.

■Although Leyland Motors Ltd had started as early as 1896, its foray into cars was much later and very brief. In 1920 the company launches the Leyland 8, a luxury touring car, a development of which is raced at Brooklands by J.G. Parry-Thomas.

LEYLAND EIGHT

The Leyland Eight was intended to be the best car in the world. It was available with either a 6,920cc engine giving 115bhp, or 7,266cc giving 145bhp, and both were overhead cam straight eights with 'hemi heads'. It also featured vacuum servo-assisted brakes, albeit only to the rear wheels. The cars were very expensive, the most expensive of their day; a bare chassis ready to go to a coachbuilder cost £2,500 in 1920, equivalent to nearly £83,000 today. Only eighteen were made between 1920 and 1923, of which one, or possibly two, survive.

1921 Ferodo introduces the first dry plate clutch with asbestos as a friction material which lasts much longer than the existing clutch materials.

■ Bentley finally starts delivery of their 3-litre model.

■ After a difficult start before the war, Aston Martin finally produces their first production car, the Standard Sports. The company had started as early as 1913 and built specials for hill climbing. The prototype of their first production car was completed in 1915, but the war put it all on ice.

■ Car Tax (the Road Fund Licence) is now set at £1 per hp. This can be paid annually or three-monthly, the payment dates being set, rather poetically, as 24 March (Spring Equinox), 30 June (Summer Solstice), 30 September (Autumn Equinox) and 31 December (Winter Solstice). Wouldn't it be rather nice if present-day tax discs referred to the equinox rather than just a numerical month?

■ Tax discs are introduced together with registration documents, or logbooks. The tax disc has never changed in size or shape since its introduction in 1921.

1922 Austin introduce the Seven, bringing motoring within the grasp of a much wider audience.

■ Marconi experiments successfully with car radios in Daimler cars, the world's first application of the radio in a self-propelled vehicle.

■ William Lyons and William Walmsley form the Swallow Sidecar Company, initially just making upmarket sidecars for motorcycles.

■ Trojan Cars finally market their first car, the prototype having been ready in 1913 before the war. It has a two-stroke, four-cylinder engine in which pairs of cylinders share a combustion chamber, and the pairs of cylinders are linked by a V-shaped connecting rod. But war got in the way of development and it was not until 1920 that the first set of cars were completed, but the final production model doesn't

AUSTIN SEVEN

The Austin Seven was, in its time, quite revolutionary, but not because of any technological features. The little car effectively wiped out the cycle cars of the early 1920s. In addition the Austin Seven effectively 'sired' BMW, its first car being a Seven made under licence, and Lotus, whose first car was a Seven special. It had a similar effect on the British car market to the effect the Ford Model T did in the States. Between 1922 and 1939, 290,000 were made. Mechanically it could hardly have been simpler, with a 747cc side-valve straight four, cable brakes and semi-elliptic springs all round.

appear until the 1922 Motor Show. The car is carried on solid tyres, unique by 1922, to prevent punctures and has very long springs to give some ride comfort.

1923 The first proper planned town bypass in Britain is opened at Eltham, now part of the A20. It will later continue as the Sidcup Bypass.

■ This year marks the first Grand Prix win by a British driver. Henry Seagrave wins the French GP at Tours in a 2-litre six-cylinder Sunbeam.

■ The number of vehicles on British roads, including motorcycles, exceeds one million for the first time.

■ Two years before being absorbed into General Motors, Vauxhall produce their finest sport car yet, the 30/98 OE.

1923 VAUXHALL 30/98 OE

The 30/98, first launched in 1913, was a sports car on a par with Bentleys. The 30/98's engine was a four-cylinder monobloc design with side valves and a capacity of 3,054cc delivering 40bhp. Although successful in competition there was a demand for more power so the engine was enlarged to 4,525cc and power was increased to 98bhp. The war interrupted production after just thirteen had been made. In 1919 production restarted as the E-type with chassis improvements but the same engine. Then in 1923 the OE-type was launched with overhead valves, a detachable cylinder head, 4,224cc and power output of 115bhp. From 1923 front brakes became available. A total of 313 OE-types were made up until 1927, the final models delivering 120bhp and excellent performance.

■ The Government's classification of roads is published. The titles Class I and Class II have changed to A and B, with lesser roads being classed as C, D or U roads, the last category being unclassified. Interestingly, the classifications C, D and U are not widely known, as they very rarely ever appeared on road signs or published maps, although they were and still are used by central and local government for planning purposes. It had been planned to include C on road signs, but the decision was quickly reversed, but not before some had been erected. Central government funding support for repairs to A and B roads is set at 60 per cent and 50 per cent respectively, the rest coming from local rates.

■ The road zones are to be defined on a radial pattern (see diagram on p.56), based on London and Edinburgh, defined by the nine principal A roads, the other roads starting with the number of the last principal road looking clockwise (so, for example, the A12 lies between the A1 and A2 arteries). The principal roads are to be:

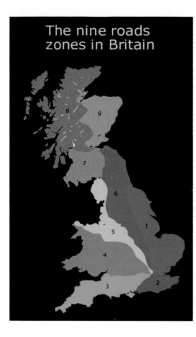

The nine roads zones in Britain

A1 London to Edinburgh
A2 London to Dover
A3 London to Portsmouth
A4 London to Avonmouth
A5 London to Holyhead

A6 Luton to Carlisle
A7 Edinburgh to Carlisle
A8 Edinburgh to Greenock
A9 Falkirk to Scrabster

■ Triumph sells its first car, the 10/20, a 1,393cc four-cylinder model. It was actually designed by Lea Francis who received a royalty on each sale. Triumph had existed since 1897 as a bicycle business and also made motorcycles from 1902. Like similar businesses, it branched out into motor cars during the 1910s and 1920s.

1924 There is some debate over when the first MG was actually built, as they started as just rebodied Morris Cowleys, but it was somewhere around 1923/24.
■ Bentley wins Le Mans for first time with their 3-litre model, driven by John Duff and Frank Clement.
■ The first one-way street system is introduced at Mare Street in Hackney. Unfortunately this predated the design of any 'one way' sign, and so instead a banner was hung across the street declaring 'One Way Traffic – No Road This Way'.
■ Frazer-Nash was founded in 1922 by Archibald Frazer-Nash, but did not begin production for sales properly until 1924–25. The first car, the Fast Tourer/Super Sports, has a four-cylinder 1.5-litre engine from Anzani. Throughout their years of production pre-Second World War, Frazer-Nash cars have either Anzani or Meadows engines, and a signature feature is their chain drive.
■ The Rootes Group has now grown to be the largest car and truck distributor in the UK.

MG EARLY SPORTS CARS

The early history of MG is quite complicated. The very first cars sold by Morris Garages (MG) were re-bodied Morris Cowleys with a few engine tweeks, as shown in the photograph. The MG 14/28, made from 1924 until 1927, had a 1,802cc side-valve four and was capable of 65mph. It sold for £350. The next model, the 14/40. was mechanically very similar to the 14/28 but now sported an MG badge on a new square radiator. Around 700 were made. The first 'true' MG is probably the 1928 18/80, which had a new purpose-built chassis and a 2.5-litre straight six with single overhead camshaft.

ROLLS-ROYCE NEW PHANTOM (PHANTOM I)

Rolls-Royce's replacement for the Silver Ghost, another 40/50, was introduced as the New Phantom in 1925. The engine was totally new, with overhead valves replacing side valves, a larger capacity of 7,668cc, the cylinders arranged as three groups of pairs and detachable cylinder heads. Up until 1931, when the Phantom II was launched, 3,512 New Phantoms were made. Rolls-Royce only ever built the chassis of the Phantom, the body being added afterwards by specialist coachbuilders. Being very expensive and long lasting, many Phantoms were later re-bodied to appear more modern.

1925 Vauxhall becomes part of General Motors and changes from being a manufacturer of high performance expensive sports cars like the 30/98 to a general producer of mid-range family automobiles.

■ Ford have sold in total 250,000 domestically produced Model Ts since 1911 from their Trafford Park factory.

■ Rolls-Royce replace the Silver Ghost with their new model, known as the New Phantom, until the Phantoms II and Phantom III came along, whereupon it became known as the Phantom I.

■ The Triumph 13/30 becomes the first British family car with hydraulic braking to all four wheels.

■ The first British dual carriageway is built at the London end of the Great West Road. There was already a single-carriageway road called the Great West Road bypassing Brentford and Hounslow and which had been built in 1920. The addition of a second carriageway turned it into the first dual-carriageway road in Britain.

■ The Criminal Justice Act 1925 makes it an offence to be drunk in charge of any mechanically propelled vehicle on the highway or any public place. The penalty is to be a fine not exceeding £50 and/or imprisonment not exceeding four months, together with a twelve-month ban from holding a licence.

■ The Invicta Company's first offering is a low-slung sporting car with a 2.5-litre straight six Meadows engine, with all round semi-elliptical springing and costing £595 (equivalent to £28,000 in today's money). Over time the marque will evolve with larger engines and even lower profiles, aided by the characteristic under-slung chassis.

1926 The government introduces the first national guidelines on where and how white lines should be painted. Before that there have been many local differences in how roads were marked.

The first dual carriageway in Britain.

■William Morris and Edward Budd, of the American Budd Corporation, set up the Pressed Steel Company to exploit steel-pressing techniques developed in the US. By the 1950s they will be producing body panels and complete bodies for most UK car manufacturers. In 1965 BMC will acquire Pressed Steel and become fully integrated. At the time it was the world's largest independent manufacturer of car bodies and car body tooling.

■The first British Grand Prix is held at the Brooklands circuit, organised by Henry Segrave. However, it was won by the French team of Louis Wagner and Robert Senechal driving a Delage 155B.

■Clyno of Wolverhampton is producing 300 cars a week and becomes the third largest car manufacturer in Britain. But by 1929 the company will cease to exist, owing to a combination of financial problems and poor sales of new models.

■Swallow Sidecars starts to build special bodies for Austin Sevens and changes its name to the Swallow Sidecar & Coachbuilding Company. Their special Austin Sevens prove very popular.

■The Rootes Group now becomes Europe's largest car distributor.

■Britain's first traffic lights are set up in Piccadilly, London. They are manually operated by a policeman.

■A petrol station opens at 9 Store Street WC1. Nothing special at the time, but it will become the first and only petrol station to be made a listed building.

■The first one-way system in Britain is introduced in Hyde Park Corner in London.

■Daimler launch their sensational Double Six.

1927 One year after the first manual lights, Britain's first set of automatic three-colour traffic lights are installed at the Prince's Square crossroads in

CLYNO CARS 1922–29

Clyno presents a sobering story for the car industry. At the peak of their short-lived success they were the third largest car manufacturer in Britain after Austin and Morris, yet today only car enthusiasts have ever heard of them. Their first car in 1922 was the 10.8hp, which sold for £250. It used a 1,368cc four-cylinder Coventry Climax engine and it was renowned for its reliability and economy. In 1924 they launched a larger model, the 13hp. However, they then embarked on a strategy of savage price reductions to undercut their competition. Although this brought spectacular growth, it put such pressure on its finances that by 1929 the company imploded and went into almost total oblivion.

DAIMLER DOUBLE SIX

Daimler's flagship model, introduced in 1926, was unusual in two ways: firstly its engine was a V12, almost unheard of at the time in road cars, and secondly it used sleeve valves rather than poppet valves. These two features made the engine exceptionally quiet and smooth, but requiring immaculate maintenance to avoid valve problems. The first Double Six had a 7,136cc 150bhp engine and as a chassis only cost £1,950. A standard saloon was available for £2,450 and a limousine for £2,800, £133,000 in today's money.

Wolverhampton. The lights, which are suspended from cables across the road, will continue in use until 1968. Initially, a policeman is stationed there to explain to motorists how they work.

■Single white lines are introduced on major roads as lane dividers to improve safety.

■The first all-steel British body is produced by Pressed Steel for the Morris Isis Six. However, after 3,939 of the original design have been produced, the all-steel body is replaced by the traditional wooden framed construction with external steel panels.

■William Morris acquires Wolseley as the motor industry starts the long march to consolidation and rationalisation, which will result in BMC and British Leyland.

■BMW, a struggling business at the time, starts manufacturing Austin Sevons under the name BMW Dixi, at first from knock-down kits then later in the year from domestically made parts. The Dixi will turn out to be the saviour of BMW.

■The world's first 'satnav' appears in the form of the British 'Plus Four Wristlet Route Indicator', a watch-like device worn on the wrist into which tiny scrolls of maps can be inserted and advanced as the journey is completed. It is not a big success.

■Triplex laminated safety glass is used for the first time in Britain on Fords.

1928 Continuing the consolidation, the Rootes Group takes over Humber, Hillman and Commer.

■Alvis announce the world's first production car with front-wheel drive and independent front suspension.

■Morris launch the Minor, the first car to use that name.

Wolverhampton's traffic lights installed in 1927.

1928 MORRIS MINOR

The Minor was launched as a rival to the highly successful Austin Seven, which had effectively created the market for small family cars. When first launched the Minor had a much more sophisticated engine, an 847cc overhead camshaft unit, whereas the Austin was a side valve. With a single SU carburettor it delivered 20bhp, enough to give the little Minor a top speed of 55mph. Later a simplified side-valve engine replaced the original model, which allowed Morris to sell the car for the 'magic' £100. The Minor survived until 1934 when it was replaced by the even more successful Eight.

1929 Clyno ceases trading after encountering financial problems and poor reception of recent models. This is just three years after being the third largest British car manufacturer.

■Armstrong Siddeley offer the Wilson pre-selector gearbox as an option, the first production car with this feature. The pre-selector gearbox is developed by Major W.G. Wilson, and he patents it in 1928. In 1929 he forms a partnership with J.D. Siddeley under the name 'Improved Gears Ltd' and it first appears on the 12hp Armstrong Siddeley model. From 1933 it becomes standard on all their models.

■Sir Denistoun Burney, the airship designer, launches his remarkable Streamline car. At 25ft long and powered by a 4-litre Beverly Barnes engine at the rear, it costs as much as a top of the range Rolls-Royce. Only twelve are made. It is said to rather resemble an airship gondola.

■The Rootes Group continues to grow by acquiring, in 1929, Hillman, Humber and Commer. They become one of the first exponents of 'badge engineering'.

■Mann and Overton, the biggest taxi dealership, sponsor Austin to create a new and much more cost-effective cab, which immediately dominates the market.

■Scammell introduce their sensational '100 Tonner', specifically designed for carrying outsize railway locomotives to port for export. It is the first vehicle ever to be able to carry 100 tons on its back, and is by far the most impressive heavy hauler of its day. With a modest 7,094cc petrol engine delivering just 86bhp, it is nonetheless able to shift 100 tons up a gradient of 1 in 10, thanks to a lowest gear ratio of 196:1. The downside: 0.75 miles per gallon and a top speed of 5mph. Just two are made, each costing £4,900 (£250,000 in today's money). One survives intact at the Leyland Museum, the other survives (just) in a breaker's yard.

Scammell's '100 Tonner' truck.

Motoring Grows Up

The 1930s showed a continuing decline in the number of car companies – a net loss of seven – and although twenty-four new businesses started, thirty-one closed down. This was mainly a continuing reflection of many start-up businesses just not being able to match up against the large manufacturers on price and quality.

Perhaps the most significant new player was a company simply called SS (1934). This, of course, would become, post-war, Sir William Lyons' Jaguar. Other significant new starters were: Burney (of Streamline fame) in 1930, Railton in 1933, Brough Superior and Squire in 1935, Jensen and HRG in 1936, Allard in 1937, and Sunbeam Talbot in 1938.

In terms of companies exiting the market, Guy disappeared as a car maker in 1932, although continuing to make trucks and buses, and Burney only survived until 1933. Lea Francis made an exit in 1935, followed by Sunbeam in 1937, Talbot in 1938 and Brough Superior in 1939.

The advent of the Second World War in 1939 put a total stop to new car businesses.

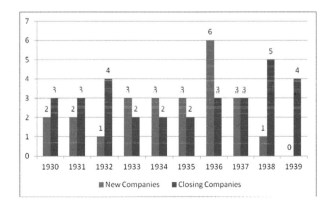

THE HISTORY OF THE DRIVING TEST

The first British person to pass a driving test was a lady called Miss Vera Hedges Butler in 1900, although she actually took a test in France, as it would be thirty-five years before a test was introduced in Britain.

In England a driving test was first introduced in 1935 – it was voluntary. The cost of the test was 37.5 pence and the pass rate was 63 per cent. The first person to pass the test was, believe it or not, a Mr Bean! As there were no test centres in 1935 the examiner and candidate would meet at a prearranged location such as a railway station. In June 1935 the test was made compulsory for anyone who started driving after 1 April 1934. There are still some people driving today who have never taken a test, although they must (by 2014) be over 96 years old.

The following is a brief timeline of the driving test:

1935: A voluntary driving test is introduced by the Road Traffic Act 1934 to avoid a rush of candidates when the test becomes compulsory. The test becomes compulsory on 1 June for all drivers who started driving on or after 1 April 1934.

1939 September: The driving test is suspended for the duration of the Second World War and does not resume until November 1946. During that time new drivers may take to the road on a provisional licence without taking a test.

1947 February: A period of a year is granted for wartime provisional licences to be converted into full licence without passing the test.

1956 November: The test is again suspended during the Suez crisis. Learners are allowed to drive unaccompanied and examiners help to administer petrol rationing.

1975: From now on candidates no longer have to demonstrate mastery of arm signals.

1990: The Driving Standards Agency (DSA) is created as an executive agency within the Department for Transport.

1991: Reverse parking manoeuvres (parallel parking) becomes a compulsory part of the test.

1995: The Pass Plus scheme is introduced to help newly qualified young drivers gain valuable driving experience and reduce the risk of being involved in an accident.

1996: A separate written theory test is introduced, replacing questions asked about the Highway Code during the practical test. The theory test must be passed before the practical test may be taken.

1997: Photograph ID is now required for both practical and theory tests, following numerous cases of people taking the test for a friend, or for a stranger for money.

1999: Cars being used for a driving test must now have front seat belts, head restraints and a rear-view mirror.

2002: A hazard perception element is introduced into the theory test. This uses video clips to test candidates' awareness of potential hazards on the road.

2003: 'Show me/tell me' vehicle safety questions are added to the beginning of the driving test.

2007: The number of theory test questions is increased from thirty-five to fifty and the new pass mark is forty-three correct answers. The pass mark for the hazard perception test for learners is forty-four out of seventy-five.

1930 The Veteran Car Club is formed after the London to Brighton Run that year when three enthusiasts meet in the bar of the Old Ship Hotel in Brighton and decide to form a club for veteran cars. Initially it was limited to cars built up to the end of 1904, but this would be extended first to 1916 and finally to 1919.

■ Third-party insurance is to become compulsory for all car drivers in the following year.

■ The Metropolitan Police introduce Britain's first police motorcycle patrols.

■ Good news for motorists, as all speed limits outside towns for ordinary cars carrying fewer than seven people are abolished under the Road Traffic Act 1930. The same Act introduces 30mph limits for coaches, buses and most heavy goods vehicles. There would be no general speed limit again for cars outside towns up until 1965.

■ Local speed limits in built-up areas can now be applied by the local authority, but these are to be 30mph, the 20mph limit being abolished.

■ The minimum age for driving is officially set at 17.

■ A test for disabled drivers is introduced, which leads to the concept of the 'invalid carriage'.

■ Road Traffic Act 1930 makes it an offence to drive, attempt to drive, or be in charge of a motor vehicle on a road or other public place while being 'under the influence of drink or a drug to such an extent as to be incapable of having proper control of the vehicle'.

■ PSV (Public Service Vehicle) licences are introduced for the first time.

1931 Compulsory motor insurance, announced in the Road Traffic Act 1930 the year before, is implemented.

■ Headlights for all cars become compulsory.

1931 JAGUAR SS1
The SS1 was the first sports car to be produced by SS Cars in Coventry. When it was launched, its looks, and low price, caused a sensation. In 1933 the company changed its name to SS Cars Ltd and then to Jaguar Cars Ltd after the war. Although sensational looking, mechanically it was quite ordinary, sporting a six-cylinder 2,054cc 48bhp or 2,552cc 62bhp Standard side-valve engine. It sold on looks and cost, not performance, 75mph being a modest speed given its sensational looks and £310 being a very low price for such glamour.

Vauxhall Cadet 2-litre.

Ford Dagenham works opened in 1931.

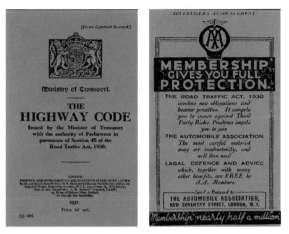

■ The Vauxhall Cadet 2-litre is the first car in Europe with a full synchromesh gearbox.

■ Bentley is acquired by Rolls-Royce. The Bentley 8-litre had been such a success as the ultimate luxury sporting car that when Napier appears interested in buying the troubled Bentley business, Rolls-Royce quickly steps in to buy the company to prevent the 8-litre continuing as a Napier-built rival for its Phantom II.

■ William Lyons launches his first in-house designed cars, the SS1 and SS2.

■ Ford begins production at their new Dagenham works, the largest car plant in Europe, but their Model A is proving very unpopular and a cloud hangs over the future of Ford in Great Britain. Design work starts on the Model Y, which would prove the salvation of Ford in Europe.

■ The first Highway Code is published, costing one penny and consisting of eighteen pages of advice. It also contained some sobering advice to errant motorists from the AA in their advertisement, as shown. The Highway Code has since grown to 135 pages.

■ The first purpose-built cross-Channel ferry is introduced. Called the Autocarrier, it was operated by Southern Railway and could carry 120 passengers and 35 cars. But rather than 'drive on' as today, the cars were loaded by crane on pallets.

1932 ASTON MARTIN LE MANS

After three business failures, Aston Martin finally got off the ground in 1932 with their Le Mans model. With its SOHC 1.5-litre engine producing 70bhp, they had a fast car capable of 85mph and 0–50mph in 16 seconds – far superior to the MGs and Singers of the time. Another feature, which would remain a feature of future Astons, was a superb exhaust note! Initially priced at a hefty £650 (£37,000 in today's money), sales were slow, but picked up after the price was dropped to £595. Only 130 were made.

1932 HILLMAN MINX

The Minx was a very conservative contender in the small family car sector. It was introduced in 1932 with a 1,185cc 30bhp engine and a pressed steel body on a separate chassis. In 1934 a four-speed box was added, as was synchromesh in 1935. A restyle in a more rounded form came in 1936, together with a new name, the Minx Magnificent. The basic format lasted until 1938 and after the war the model was briefly resurrected before a totally new Minx appeared in 1948.

Alvis Speed 20.

■ Public Service Vehicle (PSV) driver testing is introduced, but at the discretion of the local traffic commissioners.

1932 Rear-view mirrors became compulsory. It was not unknown in earlier years for drivers to carry hand mirrors and occasionally hold them up to glance behind. Lady drivers could double up their use for make-up.
■ The first pedestrian-operated street crossing lights are installed in Brighton Road, Croydon.
■ Aston Martin launch their Le Mans model.
■ Hillman introduced the popular Minx, a name which would stay with the Hillman brand until the end.
■ Alvis launch the Speed 20 as an upmarket sporting car. The photograph (left) shows the open two-seater version.
■ Ford begin production of the Model Y at Dagenham, which would prove to be immensely popular and essentially save the company.
■ The Vale Motor Company – set up in 1931 by the amazingly named Pownoll Pellew, later 9th Viscount Exmouth, as a 'gentleman's hobby' – sells its first cars in 1932. Fitted with a 832cc side-valve Triumph engine, they are desperately underpowered. This is soon to be replaced by a Coventry Climax unit, firstly a

1932 FORD 8 MODEL Y

The Ford Model Y was the first Ford designed specifically for markets outside the United States. It was a simple and robust car, powered by a 933cc 8 RAC-hp side-valve engine. It was manufactured from 1932 until 1937 and took sales from Austin, Morris, Singer and Hillman. It came in two door and four door versions, a low specification version of the former selling for just £100, the lowest priced new car ever in Britain.

1,098cc four-cylinder, and later a 1,476cc six-cylinder unit. They are noted for being low and very rakish, a victory of style over substance.

■ The first RAC Rally is staged, with the finish in Torquay. In the early days there was no overall winner.

1933 Swallow Sidecar and Coachbuilding Company formally becomes SS Cars Ltd, the precursor of Jaguar.

■ Alvis introduce the world's first all synchromesh gearbox.

■ Noel Macklin's Fairmile Engineering Company. begins making Railton cars after he sells the Invicta company. The name is derived from Reid Railton, who designed the world speed record car, but who in fact is only an advisor to the business. The first car is an Anglo-American hybrid, with a 4-litre Hudson Terraplane straight eight engine and chassis allied to British coachwork by Ranalah. Several similar Anglo-American hybrids would follow.

1936 Railton Straight Eight Sports Tourer. (Courtesy of Bryan Tyrrell)

■ Semaphore turn signals, known as 'trafficators', are introduced to replace hand signals for turning.

1934 Prior to 1934, 30mph speed limits had been at the discretion of the local authority. In 1934, the general 30mph limit in built-up areas was introduced. Interestingly, the presence of street lighting at spacing less than 100yd, without explicit 'no restriction' signs, is taken as a 30mph limit by default, a law which still applies today.

■ Morris introduce conveyor belt assembly lines at Cowley and launch the type E 8hp model.

■ Metallic finishes first become available on British cars, although they are not popular initially, most cars still being in standard black.

■ Harry Weslake joins SS Cars, later Jaguar Cars, and is one of the major influences on the design of Jaguar engines right up until the V12.

Semaphore turn signal.

1934 MORRIS E 8

The Morris 8 series E was powered by a 918cc straight-four side-valve engine delivering 23.5bhp, allowing the tourer model to reach 58mph and return 45mpg. Although the engine was very unexciting, the car did have synchromesh on the top two of its three speeds and hydraulic brakes all round, something lacking in many rivals. Prices ranged from £118 to £142. Compared to the similarly priced, lighter and longer established Austin Seven the Morris was well equipped with a full set of instruments, including speedometer, oil pressure, fuel gauges and an ammeter. Over 164,000 were made.

Morris production line at Cowley.

■ The Road Traffic Acts & Regulations 1934 give details of all approved road signs; these designs remain in use for thirty years.

■ Cat's eyes are patented. They were invented by Percy Shaw after he noticed his headlights reflected in the eyes of a cat on a dark winter night. Previous attempts by other inventors had failed, but Shaw's design was revolutionary because they were self-cleaning using rubber 'eyelids' and a self contained reservoir of rainwater collected in each unit.

■ Pedestrian crossings with flashing yellow lights are introduced by Leslie Hore-Belisha and the lights become known as Belisha beacons. At this time, however, the only markings on the road are metal studs, the 'zebra' markings come later.

■ By the mid-1930s the old registration mark system of two letters followed by four numbers is becoming exhausted in many areas, although the old system continues as late as 1963 with Bute Council. The old system is now replaced by a new three-letter plus up-to-three number system – AAA1 is issued in 1934 by Hampshire County Council. This system survives until the mid-1950s.

■ The police set up a driving school at Hendon to train police officers who use cars or motorcycles.

■ The first cycle path to separate cycles and cars is constructed on Western Avenue. However, it is not all gain for the cyclists, as they have to give way to cars turning left.

■ Philips designs and installs the first car radio as a standard fitment in the UK in the Hillman 'Melody Minx'.

■ There are now 1.5 million cars on Britain's roads, and 7,000 road deaths.

■ The first tunnel under the Mersey, the Queensway Tunnel, is opened. At 2.01 miles (3.24km) it is the longest underwater tunnel in the world, a title it will hold for twenty-four years. It has two branches leading to the dock areas on each side, one called the Rendel Street Branch (now closed) being controlled by traffic lights, a unique underwater installation at the time.

1935 Following on from the Anglo-American concept of Railton, the Brough Superior cars introduced in 1935 are similarly based on Hudson engines and chassis. The first, the 4-litre, produces 114bhp giving a top speed of 90mph and a 0–60 time of 10 seconds, sensational performance for the day.

■ Concerned about ribbon development along the increasing number of bypasses, the government passes the Restriction of Ribbon Development Act 1935.

■ William Heynes joins SS Cars Ltd as chief engineer and the SS car is announced in three sizes: 1.5 litre, 2.5 litre and 3.5 litre. The 1.5 is actually a misnomer, as the engine is 1.8 litres, but 1.5 sounded neater.

■ The Ford Model Y 8hp family car now sells for £100, equivalent to £5,700 today, and becomes the cheapest family car available.

■ 1935 marks the start of the very first driving test in Britain, which had been proposed in 1934. The test costs 37.5 pence and the pass rate is 63 per cent. Previously, a driving licence was simply purchased from a post office.

■ The first car ever to have sliding doors is a British car shown at the 1935 Motor Show.

■ Windscreen washers make their first appearance on British cars, although they would remain an expensive 'extra' for many years.

■ 1935 is the year when the concept of the London A to Z is first formulated by Phyllis Pearsall, a portrait artist who had been frustrated by the lack of a detailed street atlas when trying to find her way to a client's house at night in poor weather. She walks and maps 3,000 miles of London's streets and alleyways all on her own before producing the very first A to Z. There is some debate over how original her idea is, however.

■ L plates first appear for learner drivers, and must be displayed front and back.

1936 Morgan 4/4.

1936 Morgan introduce their first 4-wheeler.

■ William Lyons announces the sensational SS90 and SS100 sports cars, setting a tone of value, looks and performance which would continue through the XK120 and E-type. At launch the 3.5-litre version cost £395 and the 3.5-litre £445, making it the cheapest 100mph car available at the time.

■ In 1936 there are forty-five significant car manufacturers in Britain.

■ Rolls-Royce announce their new model, the Phantom III.

■ The Jensen brothers had been running a coach-building business since 1934 and in 1936 begin selling their first car, the S-Type, production having started in late 1935. The car owes its existence to the actor Clark Gable, who commissioned

Jaguar SS100.

1936 ROLLS-ROYCE PHANTOM III

The Phantom III – the final large Rolls-Royce pre-war – was extremely exclusive and was fitted with some of the most expensive coachwork ever seen on a car. It was powered by an aluminium alloy OHV 7.32-litre V12 engine, with hydraulic tappets for quietness, and had a dual ignition system, with twenty-four spark plugs, two distributors and two coils. Other advanced features included on-board jacking, a one-shot lubrication system operated from inside the driver's compartment, servo-assisted brakes and, from 1938, overdrive. Chassis production ceased in 1939 after 727 had been made. Top speed was 87mph and 0–60 could be achieved in 17 seconds, albeit at the cost of just 8mpg.

Jensen to make a car for him based around a Ford V8 chassis. It was so well received that Jenson decided to start making similar vehicles for sale.

■Ron Godfrey, Major Edward Halford and Guy Robbins form HRG in 1936, the first two partners having raced together at Brooklands, and Robbins coming from Trojan. Their first car is Meadows engined, although they switch to an overhead camshaft Singer unit in 1938. They continued making cars to an almost identical design right through to 1956, making 241 in total.

■MG launch their SA model.

■The Trunk Road Act transfers responsibility for 'major' longer-distance roads from local to central government, and introduces the suffix (T) to many A roads to denote their 'trunk' status.

1937 Speedometers become compulsory for all cars to help compliance with the 30mph speed limit.

1936 MG SA

When launched the MG SA was only available as a spacious four-door saloon, more akin to contemporary Bentleys than the open sports cars later associated with the marque. The plan had been to rival the SS cars and to encroach on Bentley territory. The car used a tuned version of the six-cylinder 2,062cc Morris engine, which it shared with the Wolseley Super Six, but enlarged to 2,288cc. The car was offered with an optional Philco radio at 18 guineas (£1,060 in today's money!) The photograph is of the attractive two-door drop-head model. A total of 2,739 were made, 350 going to Germany.

1937 LAGONDA V12

After Bentley had been taken over by Rolls-Royce, W.O. Bentley was persuaded in 1935 to join Lagonda to design new cars and also manage their racing activities. The 1937 V12 is generally considered to be his masterpiece. Its 4,480cc V12 delivered 180bhp and was so flexible it could go from 7mph to 105mph in top gear and rev to 5,000rpm. It was one of the world's most expensive cars at the time, costing up to £3,000, equivalent to around £170,000 today.

■ Lagonda launch their sensational V12, generally rated as amongst the best cars in the world in the late 1930s.

■ Percy Shaw's company Refecting Roadstuds Ltd gains its first large contract from the government for 'cat's eyes'.

■ The Chancellor of the Exchequer, Winston Churchill, removes the 'ring fence' on vehicle excise duty and from then on the duty is considered as part of general taxation. This marks the end of the 'road fund' as such, although the term road fund licence is often still used today.

■ Dipping headlights become compulsory on new cars.

■ Safety glass for windscreens and windows becomes compulsory, displacing the dangerous use of ordinary glass in cars.

■ The London Motor Exhibition is held for the first time at Earls Court rather than the Olympia.

■ Sydney Allard starts building specials for timed trials in 1937 following a formula which would be an Allard feature right to the end – a large American engine in a simple sports chassis.

1938 Petrol tax is raised from 8*d* to 9*d* per gallon, and car tax is to be calculated at £1 25s per RAC hp.

■ The Standard Flying Eight is launched as the first small British car with independent front suspension.

■ Morris launches the 8hp Series E 8, which, at £128, is the cheapest car available in Britain that year, equivalent to £6,700 in today's money.

■ SS Cars stops making automobiles and its production facilities are turned over to war production.

1938 STANDARD FLYING EIGHT

The Standard Flying Eight was a development of the 1937 Flying Nine, but with a smaller 1,021cc long-stroke engine to keep it in the 8 RAC-hp taxation bracket. With 28bhp on tap it could achieve a respectable 65mph, although with simple cable brakes, stopping was not quite so respectable. What made the Flying Eight special at the time was the use of independent front suspension, very unusual in any small car at the time, and a first in Britain.

■A plan is published (as shown on p.73) portraying how motorways might look in the future. It is notably different from what actually came about, especially as it shows a north–south motorway parallel with the Welsh border, and another north/south cutting across the M4 near Reading.

■Sir Charles Bressey and Sir Edwyn Lutyens publish a Ministry of Transport report: 'The Highway Development Survey 1937.' The report reviews London's road needs and recommends the provision of a series of orbital roads, the first suggestion of an M25-type concept.

■The car tax disc is perforated for the first time.

■The first car badged as a Sunbeam Talbot, the Ten, is launched in 1938, based on Hillman and Humber components. Both Sunbeam and Talbot had been well-established concerns before 1938, when they were both purchased by the Rootes Group and the new marque was created.

1939 Wartime restrictions require headlamps to be masked and streetlights turned off. The adverse effect on road safety results in more people killed on the roads than in conflict during the first six months of the Second World War, with 8,272 deaths on the roads in 1939.

■All driving tests are suspended during hostilities.

■Petrol rationing is introduced, allowing enough petrol for around 200 miles per month per car.

■Many road projects, and in particular bypasses, are put on hold. Many have been started, as well as lots of bridges and earthworks built, but will not be finished until the 1960s.

■Insurers complain that the incidence of car accident injury claims is increasing at such a rate (largely due to the blackout) that it is putting a strain on resources.

■Car ownership stands at 10 per cent of households.

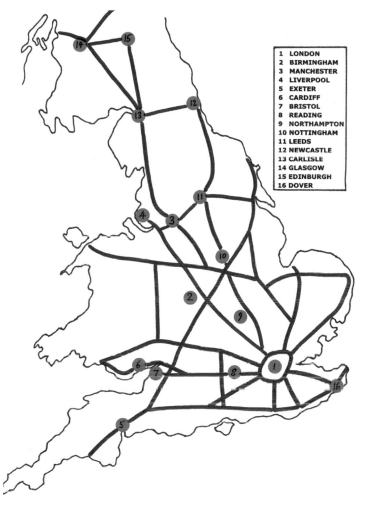

The distinct 1930s-style bridge on the Northwich bypass. The road across the bridge was not completed until the late 1960s, and even then came to a sudden stop. The bypass was not completely finished until the mid-1970s.

Wartime and Austerity

The 1940s was dominated by the Second World War; even after war finished in 1945, manufacturing industries were still severely restricted in terms of raw materials and the desperate need to export to repay mainly American loans. It was the quietest decade ever for British car manufacturing. Ironically, recycled aluminium was quite readily available, which favoured the small specialist manufacturers, including Land Rover, whereas steel was in very short supply.

The most significant new business was Jaguar, founded in 1945, and reflected in the demise of the former SS Cars, whose name was now unacceptable, for obvious reasons. Other significant new ventures were Bristol and Healey in 1946 and Land Rover and Bond in 1948.

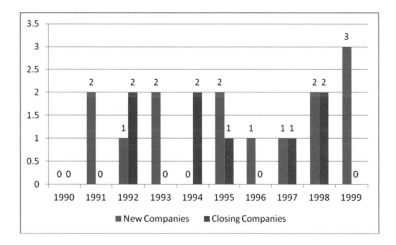

HISTORY OF BRITISH CAR NUMBER PLATES

The requirement for a vehicle in Britain to display a registration mark started in 1904. The purpose was to help in the identification of vehicles in case of accidents, theft or contravention of motoring laws. Registration marks have passed through five different protocols:

Prior to 1932: Registration marks consisted of one or two letters followed by up to four numbers, so the full series ran from A 1 through to YY 9999. The letters 'Z', 'I' and 'Q' were not used in case of confusion with '2', '1' and the letter 'O' or, additionally, in the case of 'I' and 'Z', reserved for use in Northern Ireland. The initial letters were assigned on the basis of population size of the registering area according to the 1901 Census. So 'A' meant London, 'B' meant Lancashire, 'C' the West Riding of Yorkshire, and so on. Scotland and Northern Ireland had a different series starting with the letters 'S' and 'I' respectively. When each authority had used up all combinations with one letter plus numbers up to 9999, then a second letter was added and the sequence continued. The second letters were added on a 'first come first served' basis.

1932–63: By 1932 the numbers available under the first system, which totalled 5,289,471, were starting to run out. So an extended protocol was introduced, whereby three letters and three numbers were used, ranging from 'AAA 1' to 'YYY 999'. The three letters continued to reflect the issuing authority, the second and third letters continuing as before 1932, with the additional letter added as a prefix. However, the very rapid growth in car registrations meant that this new system would run out within ten years.

1963–02. By 1963 the new numbering system was becoming exhausted. The new idea was to add a 'date letter', which would help in two ways: it would give car buyers an immediate knowledge of a car's age and would also help the police to make a rough check of the registration mark against the obvious age of a car, thereby reducing the risk of number plate theft. The system of using three

letters plus up to three numbers, and also a suffix date letter, was introduced. Some authorities still had old registrations to use up and did not follow the 'date letter' idea until 1966, when it became compulsory. Initially the 'date letter' changed on 1 January each year, but car retailers were concerned that this end of year change had a disproportionate effect on car sales; therefore, in 1967 the 'date letter' change was moved to August so that each calendar year embraced two letters.

1983–2001: The existing system was time bound rather than sales bound and by 1983 the date letters had reached 'Y', and as 'Z' was never used as a date letter a further change was needed. The new protocol simply reversed the existing system, with a 'date letter' followed by up to three numbers and then three letters. So the available range became 'A21 AAA' through to 'Y999 YYY', the numbers 1–20 initially being held back for the proposed DVLA registration sales scheme, which was later implemented. The 1983 change also brought into use the prefix letter 'Q', which was reserved for vehicles of indeterminate age, such as kit cars and imports. With the added complexity of registration marks a new problem arose: the increasing risk of registrations spelling out obscene or unacceptable words. So the DVLA introduced a committee to oversee all possible new marks and filter out those that might cause offence.

2001–Present: In September 2001 a totally new system was introduced, which it was hoped would remove the peak in sales around the date letter change and also introduce a type of mark that might be easier for witnesses to hit-and-run accidents and other offences to remember. The new format is two letters, followed by two numbers and ending with three letters. The first two letters relate to the region of registration, the two numbers identify the date of registration, but in a less than obvious form, and the last three letters are random.

When the current system runs out some new combination will have to be devised. Out of interest, the system described here was a strictly British, rather than a UK, system. Northern Ireland has continued to use a three-letter plus four-number system, where the first letter has always been 'I'.

1940 Under the direction of General Edmund Ironside concentric rings of anti-tank defences and pillboxes are constructed round London. These consist of the London Inner Keep, London Stop Line Inner, London Stop Line Central and the Outer London Ring. These are not roads, of course, but are significant as the M25 from Watford to Chigwell actually follows the route of the Outer London Ring. Many defences are still visible but more lie buried now under the M25.
■ A 20mph limit is introduced for night-time driving in built-up areas in an attempt to reduce fatalities during the blackout.
■ British Summer Time is first introduced to try to further reduce the death toll on the roads.

1941 In 1941 there are 9,169 deaths of the roads, including 4,781 pedestrians. The deaths are 38 per cent higher than before the war in spite of just half number of cars actually being on the road.

1942 The idea of 'curb drill' for safe road crossing is introduced.

1945 The end of the war leaves a car industry drained of resources and with little hope of producing new models for several years.
■ The Triumph Motor Company is acquired by Standard.
■ To help the economy recover from the war and repay foreign debts, British car manufacturers are required to export at least half their production.
■ The New Car Covenant is implemented, whereby new car buyers must sign a document agreeing not to sell a new car for at least one year to avoid black market profiteering.
■ Most car manufacturers have little choice but to resume building pre-war models, including Austin with their 1932-designed 10hp and 1939-designed 8hp and Jaguar with their pre-war SS models, now called Jaguars.

1946 As a first sign of the relaxation of austerity, the petrol ration is increased by 50 per cent, allowing around 300 miles per month for the average car.
■ Ford Britain produces its millionth car in the UK at Dagenham, a cream-coloured Ford 10 Saloon.
■ With an optimistic view of the future, the government publishes a map of a proposed network of new 'motorways', including the M1, M4, M5, M6, M62,

M18 and M25, although it would be twelve years before any of it even starts. In fact, this plan is identical to the one published before the war in 1938.

■ Driving tests, which had been suspended during the war, are resumed.

■ New post-war models appear from Triumph, Armstrong Siddeley, Jowett and Bentley.

■ Bristol launch the 400.

■ The Triumph 1800 roadster becomes the first British car with a steering column gear change and also features a 'dickey seat' in the boot, the last car to be equipped with this feature. It is sometimes called the 'mother-in-law' seat, as the occupants have to sit out in the elements even when the roof is up.

■ Daimler introduce the DE36.

1946 BRISTOL 400

Bristol acquired BMW designs and tooling as part of the war reparations in 1945–46. In 1947 they built the prototype 2-litre 400 model based on the BMW 326, 327 and 328. It featured a slightly modified version of BMW's six-cylinder 1,971cc engine delivering 80bhp, and making the 400 capable of 92mph. The engine had hemispherical combustion chambers requiring complex valve gear involving pushrods, followers and bell-cranks. It was a powerful and efficient engine but required very careful maintenance. Around 700 of these new Bristols were built before 1950, and they remain the only Bristols ever built with steel bodies.

1946 DAIMLER DE36

The DE36 was one of the very last straight-eight cars in the world. Powered by a 5,460cc eight developing 150bhp, driving through a fluid flywheel and pre-selector gearbox, it was simultaneously a superlative vehicle for royalty and a symbol of outrageous decadence. Of the 216 built, seven were drop-head coupés made famous by Sir Bernard and Lady Docker and generally known as 'Green Goddesses'. These were outrageously extravagant and expensive cars used mainly by Sir Bernard's ex-showgirl wife Norah. The cars and the negative publicity surrounding them cost the company a great deal, made the Dockers a source of ridicule and ultimately cost Sir Bernard Docker his job as chairman of BSA and Daimler.

1946 JOWETT JAVELIN

So soon after the war, when many manufacturers were still serving up reheated pre-war cars, the Javelin was a bold technological step forward. It had a flat-four twin carburettor overhead valve 1,486cc engine with an aluminium block and wet liners. With 50bhp it was capable of 77mph. The earlier models had hydraulic tappets, like the Phantom III, torsion bar suspension on all wheels, which was independent at the front, and rack and pinion steering. Although 23,000 were sold, it was seen as too 'different' by many and expensive, too, at £819.

■Donald Healey founds the Healey Motor Company in 1945 and the first Healey models, the Westland Roadster and Elliott Saloon, are launched in 1946, both with 2.4-litre six-cylinder Riley engines.
■Standard and Triumph merge to form Standard-Triumph.

1947 The Transport Act 1947 nationalises all British bus companies.
■Jowett launch the idiosyncratic Javelin.
■The Act also nationalises the road haulage business under the Transport Commission. The resulting organisation is called British Road Services. It will eventually be privatised to its employees under the Conservative government of Margaret Thatcher to become the National Freight Consortium.
■A period of one year's grace is granted to holders of wartime provisional licences to convert to a full licence without having to take a test.
■The RAC/ACU (Auto Cycle Union) Motorcycle Training Scheme is introduced to improve safety.
■David Brown, the tractor tycoon, buys Aston Martin for £20,500 and Lagonda the following year for £52,500, leading to the DB range of models. This saves the two companies from extinction.
■The name Vanguard appears on Standard's new model.
■It is announced that, with effect from next year, car tax will be simplified to a flat rate of £10, removing the extra burden on larger engined cars caused by the RAC hp formula.
■Ford launch the Pilot.

1947 STANDARD VANGUARD

The name Standard Vanguard was a reference to HMS *Vanguard*, the last of the Royal Navy battleships which had been launched in 1944, and the use of this name involved lengthy negotiations with the Royal Navy and Admiralty. The new car cost £543 and its distinctly transatlantic appearance was not universally popular. Power came from a 2,088cc straight four and it was capable of 79mph, 0–60 in 24 seconds and around 23mpg. Suspension at the front was independent and front and rear had anti-roll bars. From 1949 an overdrive became an option at a cost of £45. The basic car cost £671.

1947 FORD V8 PILOT

The Pilot was in many ways an odd choice for austerity Britain, with its 3,622cc side-valve V8 engine and pre-war transatlantic looks. It was seen as dated when launched and initially underpowered, with a 2,227cc engine, which was soon replaced by the larger unit. Vacuum powered windscreen wipers, cable rear brakes, 6-volt electrics and vague worm and roller steering added to the dated feel. Performance was reasonable, with a top speed of 80mph and 0–60mph in 21 seconds, although 18mpg was the price to be paid. However, it proved very popular and 22,155 were sold by 1951.

■ Austin starts building a range of luxury cars, starting with the A110/A120 Sheerline and A135 Princess – expensive cars for a country recovering from war.
■ Austin launch a new, more modern-looking range, starting with the A40 Devon.
■ The last horse-drawn hackney carriage is withdrawn from the streets of London.
■ A new Austin taxi, the FX3, appears on the market. The design of the FX3 is still considered to be the look of the traditional London taxi.

1948 New cars start to appear, although in small quantities because of steel shortages. Some customers could expect to wait six years for delivery because most cars are still exported.

1948 MORRIS MINOR

The Morris Minor was born in 1948 as the MM series, which continued until 1953. It was an advanced car for its time in many ways, with almost unitary construction, rack and pinion steering and independent front suspension by torsion bars. It had been designed originally for a flat four engine, but later in development this was changed to a 918cc side-valve straight four taken from the outgoing Morris 8, which delivered 27.5bhp and allowed 64mph and 40mpg. The Minor quickly developed, acquiring an OHV engine in 1952 and increased capacity of 948cc in 1956, when it became known as the Minor 1000. In total 1.3 million Minors were made, of which 850,000 were Minor 1000s.

1948 JAGUAR XK120

When launched in 1948 the XK120 was a sensation, as the E-type would be years later. A superb looking car, at a reasonable price, and capable of 120mph, it was bound to be a hit as the world's fastest production car. The famous XK engine – a DOHC 3.4-litre twin-carburettor unit delivering 160bhp – was making its first appearance. A 0–60mph time of just 10 seconds was remarkable for 1948. The first 242 cars were built with handmade aluminium bodies over an ash frame before switching to steel as demand rose.

■ The 1948 Standard Vanguard is the first car in Europe to be offered with an overdrive unit, made by Laycock de Normanville (later GKN Laycock).
■ The first post-war motor show is held at Earls Court.
■ Morris introduce the legendary Minor.
■ Jaguar release their first new post-war model, the Mk V, still with the pre-war side-valve standard 3.5-litre engine. The old SS saloons are then often referred to as Mk IVs.
■ Jaguar stun the motoring world by announcing the sensational XK120 with the new XK engine.

Silver City's cross-Channel air service starts.

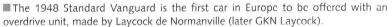

1948 LAND ROVER

The 1948 Land Rover gave birth to the whole 4x4 market both here in Britain and abroad. The 1948 Series 1 was designed for farm and light industrial use initially. At first there was just one model, an 80in wheelbase with a 1.6-litre petrol engine producing 50bhp. The four-speed box from the Rover P3 was used, together with a new two-speed transfer box. Initially the Land Rover has an unusual four-wheel-drive system with a freewheel, as on most Rovers of the time, but by 1952 a 2-litre engine and a proper full four-wheel-drive system was adopted.

■The iconic Land Rover is launched, a design which continues in spirit to this day with the Defender.

■Allard start producing fast V8-powered sports cars in the same vein as the pre-war Anglo-American hybrids like Railton and Brough.

■Silver City launches its cross-channel car air ferry using a Bristol 170 Freighter. It flies from Lympne in Kent to Le Touquet and carries three cars. At the beginning the one-way fare for a car with four passengers was £32, equivalent to £961 today. In 1948 they carried only 178 cars. By the following year they would be operating five aircraft on the route, carrying 2,700 cars and 10,000 passengers.

■This year the Vincent Black Lightning motorcycle is launched. Extremely expensive and extremely fast, only thirty-one are eventually made. However, it is notable for one amazing fact: each model is tested on the Great North Road near the Stevenage factory to guarantee it is capable of 150mph and each one sold

1949 ROVER P4

The P4 75 appeared in 1949 and launched the 'aunty' image which Rover would keep until the launch of the P6 in 1963. It featured controversial modern styling, which contrasted with the outdated Rover P3 that it replaced. One particularly unusual feature was the centrally mounted headlight in the grille, which disappeared after 1952. Power came from a 2,103cc IOE straight-six engine. A four-speed manual transmission was used with a column gear change at first and a floor-mounted unit from 1954. It had a top speed of 84mph and could accelerate from 0–60mph in 21.6 seconds, returning 28mpg. The basic 75 cost £1,106 including taxes.

bears a brass plaque recording the event. This was at a time when the average family car struggled to get above 65mph.

1949 The Special Roads Act 1949 gives highway authorities powers for the first time to restrict some roads to certain classes of traffic only, making them not public rights of way anymore and with access restricted to a few specially constructed interchanges. It is proposed that these powers will be used first on the Slough and Maidenhead bypasses as 'Trunk Road Motorways', the precursor of the motorways and motorway traffic restrictions we know today.

■ In a bid to gain a bigger foothold in the US, Austin launch the A90 Atlantic with bold styling designed to appeal to the American market. But, with its large four-cylinder engine, it is not a big success in a market used to big lazy V8s.

■ The Institute of Advanced Motorists is formed.

■ Rover launch the P4.

The Post-War Gloom Starts to Lift

This decade saw a recovery in activity in the industry after the war. Over the whole decade thirty new businesses started up and twenty-two closed down, giving a net growth of the industry of eight car companies. Amongst new starters were Lotus in 1951, Austin Healey and Reliant, both in 1952, and Sunbeam in 1953.

The decade also saw a number of specialist and kit car companies start up, including Ginetta in 1957, Elva in 1958 and Marcos and Gilbern in 1959. The Isle of Man-based Peel, noted for producing the world's smallest car, started production in 1955.

Many well-known names disappeared during the decade, including Invicta and Railton in 1950, Lea Francis in 1952, Healey, Jowett and Sunbeam Talbot in 1954, HRG and Lanchester in 1956, Frazer Nash in 1957 and Connaught in 1959. These were all victims of the scale economies achieved by the larger manufacturers.

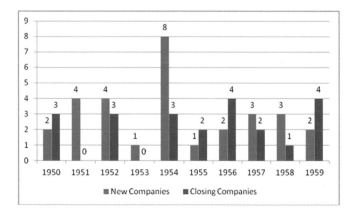

THE HISTORY OF ROAD SIGNS

The Romans were the first to use road signs in Britain. Some Roman milestones still survive, but all traces of their other signs, such as direction signs made of timber, have long since vanished.

Before 1648 any road signs which were put up were local private initiatives. They were hardly needed, as most people only travelled as far as they could walk, and they knew where they were going.

In 1648 a law was passed requiring every parish to install guide posts or finger posts at all crossroads.

The General Turnpike Act of 1773 made the turnpike trusts responsible for finger posts at all important junctions, and for milestone to help with the calculation of tolls.

From the mid-nineteenth century the arrival of canals and railways introduced many bridges onto our roads. These often had weight restrictions on them and the railway and canal companies would install signs themselves, many of which still survive.

During the second half of the nineteenth century, caution signs were erected to warn cyclists of sharp bends and steep hills. Before bicycles became popular roads were only used by pedestrians, people on horseback and horse-drawn vehicles, and, with nothing exceeding 10mph, signs were scarcely necessary.

With the arrival of the motor car, the newly formed motoring organisations started to put up their own signs, the RAC from 1897 (blue) and the AA from 1905 (yellow).

In 1903 the Motor Car Act made legislative provision for local authorities to erect their own warning signs, which were then standardised and defined in a circular published in 1904. A hollow red triangle meant a hazard, a solid red disc a prohibition, a hollow white ring a speed limit and a red diamond shape was information. It is ironic that most cars didn't have speedometers in 1903, so the speed limit sign would have been of limited effectiveness.

In 1921, following a review of signage, a limited number of signs was introduced incorporating symbols as well as text. Some were particularly and uniquely British, such as the 'flaming torch of knowledge' for a school.

In 1933 a committee chaired by Brigadier-General Sir Henry Maybury introduced the first formal official signs, including 'No Entry' and 'Keep Left'.

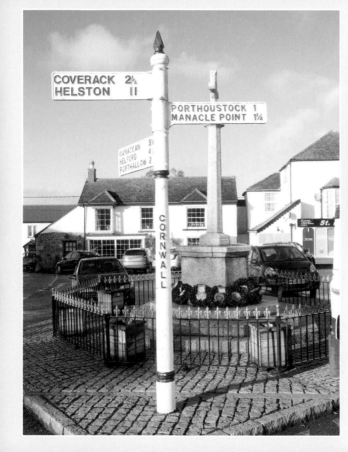

'Pre-Warboys' 'finger-post' signage.

In 1934 the government published the *Road Traffic Acts and Regulations* handbook, which further standardised signs and also saw the end of permanent AA signs, although the RAC continued to erect signs to these standards, but without the RAC logo. The 1934 designs continued up until 1964.

1934 also saw the first signs which incorporated information within the sign, so the new 30mph sign had the '30' inside the red 'order' ring. Also the 'Halt' sign was unique in being T-shaped.

In 1939 many road signs were removed in case of invasion.

The next major change came with the arrival of motorways. In anticipation of the opening of the first motorway, the M6 Preston bypass, Jock Kinneir and Margaret Calvert from the Chelsea School of Art are asked by the Anderson Committee in 1957 to create new signs appropriate for the new high-speed roads.

In 1958 these new signs were tested on the new stretch of M6. The signs were innovative in using upper and lower case letters.

Following the success of the new motorway signs, the Warboys Committee commissions Kinneir and Calvert to overhaul all of Britain's road signs. The new signs became law in 1965. These signs were standardised with triangles for warnings, circles for commands and rectangles for information and were compatible with continental European signage.

An interesting point of trivia: Calvert disliked the existing school sign, saying it had overtones of 'grammar school pupils', so she produced a new one with a girl leading a smaller boy. The girl was apparently a simplified self-portrait and the cow on the farm sign was based on one at a relative's farm.

With their new signs, the duo invented two new fonts: 'Transport' and 'Motorway'. These two fonts are still the only ones permitted on British road signs.

The only major changes since 1965 have been the addition of new signage, including the brown tourist signs, holiday routes, electronic signs, colour coding for routes and variable mandatory speed limits.

The Warboys Committee published its findings in the Traffic Signs Regulations and General Directions (TSRGD), which continues to be the 'bible' for British road signs.

1950 Petrol rationing, which had been introduced in 1939 at the start of the war, is finally removed. However, the motorist couldn't win: the fuel tax is doubled.

■ The New Car Covenant, which obliged purchasers of new cars to keep them for at least one year before selling them to avoid a 'black market' for cars, is tightened up. Owners now have to keep their new cars for two years not one – not that there were many new cars to buy anyway.

■ A small piece of good news for the wealthier car buyers: the purchase tax on luxury cars is halved.

■ The pass rate on the driving test is 50 per cent in 1950, significantly better than it is today, but down from when the test was first introduced.

■ More good news for the super-super-rich: Rolls-Royce announce the Phantom IV, the last straight eight production car in the world. The only snag is that you need more than just money to get one. Just eighteen are to be built and they are to be exclusively reserved for royalty and heads of state – oh, and General Franco in Spain 'bagged' no less than three of them!

■ Rover unveil to the world the very first gas turbine car: the rear-engined two-seater JET 1. The big question was would it herald the dawn of a new era in motoring or just introduce a new way of singeing pedestrians' eyebrows. The rev counter would also have taken some getting used to, peak revs being 52,000.

■ Ford introduces its new range of upper-middle-market models: the Consul and Zephyr. The Zephyr looks set to keep the chromium plating industry alive and make lots of middle management happy. Middle management with aspirations might hanker after the even flashier Zephyr Zodiac.

Rover JET 1.

1950 FORD CONSUL ZEPHYR

The Ford Zephyr range, consisting of the Consul, Zephyr and Zephyr Zodiac, was introduced in 1950 as replacements for the Ford Pilot. They were the first mass-production cars to use McPherson strut front suspension. The Zephyr was a lengthened version of the four-cylinder 1,508cc Consul, using a 2,262cc six-cylinder engine delivering 68bhp. It was capable of 80mph, 0–60 in 20.2 seconds whilst returning 23mpg. The Zephyr Six was quite a tough vehicle, with one winning the Monte Carlo Rally in 1953. Prices started at around £842.

■Jensen launch their first proper post-war car, the Interceptor, based largely on Austin Sheerline components.

■The total number of motor vehicles in Britain tops 2.5 million, and people are already starting to wonder if there's room for all of them.

■The Paramount is a most unusual venture in 1950. With a wood-frame body and aluminium bodywork, it is very well built but suffered from serious technical shortcomings. Suspension front and rear is by leaf springs and the engine, a Ford 10 1,172cc side-valve unit, is grossly inadequate. A plan to use an Alvis engine and suspension was dropped on cost grounds. At £1,009 (£23,000 in today's money) it is very expensive for what it offered – basically a fancy small Ford side valve – and production will cease in 1956 after just seventy have been made.

■In 1950 the European system of 'E routes' is introduced to define pan-European roads. Britain has never shown the E number on roads, although they do exist. The E22 for example includes the route from Holyhead to Hull as part of a Dublin to Denmark 'super highway'. Similarly, the Glasgow to Madrid route, the E05, includes all of the M6. Somehow, though, it's just not British – to most of us 'E numbers' are things you find on processed food packages. Almost nobody has heard of these European 'E routes'.

1951 The distinctive 'zebra' markings are introduced on pedestrian crossings, which had first appeared in 1934 without them. So, 'Belisha beacons' now became 'zebra crossings'. The first zebra crossing is installed in Slough on the High Street, one of the few positive things about Slough.

■Colin Chapman founds Lotus Engineering, with an emphasis on lightweight cars with small, efficient engines. He had built one-off specials since 1948, starting with the Lotus Mk 1. His formula of extreme lightweight and small efficient engines would be an enduring feature of all their models.

■Jaguar launch the C-type as their big hope in sports-car racing, in particular with an eye on winning Le Mans.

■Turner sports cars go on sale, two years after the Turner Sports Car Company was established. A total of 670 of his lightweight sports cars will be built with a variety of engines, including Ford, MG, Lea Francis and Vauxhall.

■From the early 1950s three-lane roads start to become popular as a way of coping with more traffic. However, they are only safe with low volumes of traffic and they became notorious by the late '60s. It was said at the time that the three lanes are a left side, a right-side and a sui-cide.

AUSTIN A30

The A30 was Austin's answer to the Morris Minor and was the first Austin to have full monocoque construction. Introduced as the new Austin Seven, at £507 it undercut the Minor by £62. Evidence of strict cost cutting could be seen in the fact that only one windscreen wiper and one sun visor were standard, the others being extras. Its newly designed A-series straight-four OHV engine was state of the art in 1951, although it was forced to be offered with relatively low compression ratio because of the quality of petrol in 1951, just 70 octane; so, top speed was 62mph and 0–60 in a sedate 42 seconds.

■ The first RAC Rally since the war sees the best performance by Ian Appleyard in a Jaguar XK120.
■ Austin launch the A30.

1952 British Motor Corporation (BMC) is formed by the merger of the Nuffield organisation and Austin Motors. Its symbol becomes the famous BMC rosette.
■ The Austin Healey marque is created by a joint venture between BMC and Donald Healey to develop fast two-seater sports cars in a very British vein.
■ Equipped with the new revolutionary Dunlop disc brakes, Jaguar C-types take 1st, 2nd and 4th at Le Mans.
■ Bentley introduce the R-type to replace the Mk 6. Since the Mk VI, Bentley and Rolls-Royce have simply been exercises in badge engineering and the Rolls-Royce Silver Dawn also acquires the 'big boot' look of the R-type.
■ Bentley also introduce the sensational R-type Continental, the fastest full four-seater in the world at the time.
■ The Armstrong Siddeley Sapphire, and later Star Sapphire, are introduced as the last luxury offerings from the company before production ceases in 1960.

1953 With the legacy of wartime austerity fading, higher-octane fuels become available, allowing higher compression engines and more power. Up until 1945, 100-octane petrol was channelled almost exclusively for aero engine use and in

BENTLEY R-TYPE CONTINENTAL

In spite of its name, the Continental was produced mainly for the UK market, 80 per cent being produced in right-hand drive. The chassis was a modified R-type with some tuning modifications to the carburettors and inlet and exhaust manifolds. Production started in 1952 and in 1954 the engine was enlarged from 4,566cc to 4,887cc and the compression ratio was raised. All Continentals had coach-built bodywork, the majority by H.J. Mulliner. The Continental was the fastest four-seater car in the world at the time, being capable of 117mph and 0–60 in 13.8 seconds. It was also one of the most expensive, costing around £7,600, equivalent to £181,000 today.

the early post-war years 72-octane 'pool' petrol was the norm. Now 80- and 90-octane appear at the pumps.

■The Triumph TR2 and Healey 100/4 are launched, offering 100mph in reasonably priced sports cars, just one step down from an XK120.

■Singer announce the SMX Roadster, Britain's first plastic-bodied production car. But driving around in a glorified plastic bag clearly doesn't appeal to many British drivers and only twelve are sold.

■Radial ply and tubeless tyres make their first appearance: radials are introduced by Michelin and tubeless tyres by Dunlop.

TRIUMPH TR2

The TR2 was designed to compete against MG. Standard already made the Roadster, but that was out of date and underpowered; the company now wanted an affordable, fast sports car. The chassis was a shortened version of that of the Standard Eight, and used a twin carburettor version of the 1,991cc Standard Vanguard engine, turning out 90bhp. Between 1953 and 1955, 8,636 were produced, of which 377 were still licensed in 2011. It was a fast car capable of 107mph and 0–60 in 12 seconds, returning around 29mpg. The car cost around £900, with an overdrive operating on all gears adding another £56.

Nash Metropolitan.

■The Austin Healey 100S becomes the first serial production car in the world with disc brakes on all four wheels.

■The New Car Covenant purchase scheme, introduced after the war to prevent new cars being resold at a premium on the black market, is finally abolished.

■The Nash Metropolitan is launched. This car was designed for the US market, but Nash had decided the costs of tooling for the new car in the States would be prohibitive and so decided to look abroad for a company who could make the car using largely existing components, and chose Austin. This production overseas is a forerunner of what has become common these days, especially with Nissan, Toyota and Honda building cars in the UK.

■For the first time the RAC Rally declares an outright winner – Ian Appleyard in a Jaguar XK120.

1954 The Lanchester Sprite becomes the first volume production car in Britain to be offered with automatic transmission.

■The Standard Vanguard Phase II is the first British car to be offered with a diesel option. The engine had been developed for Ferguson tractors, but with the rev limiter removed power leaps from 22bhp to 60bhp, giving a top speed of just 66mph and 0–60mph in 31.6 seconds. It wasn't cheap either at £1,099, but 1,973 were sold to those with tough eardrums and big wallets, who were not in a hurry.

■Jaguar replace the XK120 with the new XK140, and for sports-car racing the C-type is replaced by the D-type, although in its first year it does not win at Le Mans.

AUSTIN A40 CAMBRIDGE

The 1956 A40 Cambridge replaced the A40 Somerset and was Austin's second unitary construction car. It was powered by a similar 1.2-litre OHV four, as used in the earlier car, but now delivering 42bhp. It was capable of 79mph and accelerated from 0–60 in 27 seconds, returning around 29mpg. The A40 Cambridge only lasted until 1957, by which time just 30,000 had been built. It was replaced by the A50, and later the A55 and A60. The title A40 was then used for the smaller Farina-styled car, the Countryman version of which was Britain's first hatchback.

■Austin introduce the A40 Cambridge with unitary construction, replacing the separate chassis A40 Somerset.

■There is the first major revision of the Highway Code.

■Although the Preston Bypass (M6) will be the first stretch of motorway to open, it is not the first section of motorway to be built. In 1954 Lancashire County Council is offered a large amount of hardcore waste by a quarrying company near Manchester and they use it to construct the two embankments leading to the Barton Bridge over the Manchester Ship Canal. By the time the bridge is completed the route will have been upgraded and will form part of the M62, making the embankments the oldest motorway construction in the country.

■Flashing direction indicators become legal. However, many people do not like them, thinking them 'too American', and wish to hang on to the old semaphore-arm signals.

1955 Jaguar launch the iconic 2.4 and 3.4 sports saloons, which become known retrospectively as the Mk1 once the Mk2 is launched.

■Jaguar win Le Mans with the greatly improved D type.

■Bentley and Rolls-Royce replace the R-type and Silver Dawn with the S1 and Silver Cloud respectively, but still with the same 4.9-litre six. However, the S1 and Cloud come with automatic transmission as standard, although a manual may still be specified, but rarely is.

■Jensen launch the sensational 541 with a fibreglass body and backbone chassis, whose hollow tubes are used as the vacuum reservoir for the brakes. However, like the Interceptor, it is still based on Austin Sheerline mechanicals.

Rolls-Royce Silver Cloud.

■By the mid-1950s the registration marks for cars are changed – from three letters followed by three numbers to three numbers followed by three letters.

■The Peel Engineering Company, which was making fibreglass boats and fairings for motorcycles, launches the Peel Trident and P50 microcars, the only cars ever made on the Isle of Man and the smallest production road cars in the world, even to this day.

■The League of Safe Drivers is formed. In 1980 it will become amalgamated with the RoSPA.

■Dunlop now has half the British tyre market.

■MG launch the MGA.

MGA

The MGA was MG's move away from the traditional T-type cars, with their separate wings and running boards. With a totally new chassis, and the new BMC B-series engine, the new car was much more modern and sleek. The 1,489cc engine produced 68bhp – soon uprated to 72bhp – the top speed was 97.8mph, with acceleration from 0–60 taking 16 seconds, and fuel consumption was 27mpg. The standard car cost £844. In 1958 a high-performance twin-cam version was introduced, offering 108bhp, a top speed of 113mph and 0–60 in just 9.1 seconds. However, the engine proved troublesome at the time and the twin-cam model was not a success. A total of 58,750 were made, the vast majority being exported.

1956 After a most distinguished history of automotive innovation starting in 1895, Daimler finally pulls the plug on the Lanchester name, ceasing production of the Lanchester Sprite.

■ BMC commissions Pininfarina to redesign its range of medium-sized saloons, which would result in the iconic 'fin tail' Austin, Morris, Wolseley and MG ranges.

■ The Jaguar D-type wins Le Mans for second time.

■ Charles Cross petrol station in Plymouth is claimed to be the first purpose-built self-service petrol station in Britain. On the basis that it wasn't totally self-service, and was actually indoors, another claimant to be the first 'modern-style' self-service petrol station, appears in 1961.

■ The first 'yellow lines' to restrict parking appears in Slough, Berkshire – another moment of fame for Slough.

■ The Suez crisis seriously limits supplies of oil and petrol and wartime-style rationing is introduced again. Using coupons based on car registration plates, there is a limit of 10 gallons per month.

■ Driving tests are temporarily suspended again. Anyone who has held a licence for one month during the crisis is allowed to drive unaccompanied for the time being.

■ Petrol rationing results in an upsurge of interest in 'micro cars', such as the awful Rodley and dreadful Fairthorpe Atom. The world would have to wait three more years for the Mini to appear to kill off this most unfortunate segment of the market.

■The Montagu Motor Museum opens at Palace House in Beaulieu, building on the existing collection of Lord Montagu.

■Berkeley start production of their lightweight glass-fibre monocoque car a year ahead of the Lotus Elite with similar construction. The early cars have an air-cooled twin-cylinder Anzani engine of 322cc or 328cc. In spite of the tiny engine the car has good performance owing to its extremely light-weight.

■Institute of Advanced Motorists introduces the Advanced Driving Test.

■The Road Traffic Act 1956 makes the 30mph limit in built-up areas permanent.

■The first of the iconic Routemaster buses enter service in London.

1957 Lotus launch the Elite with glass-fibre monocoque construction, similar to that of the Berkeley launched the previous year, although actual sales will not start until 1958.

■Jaguar continues the evolution of their sports car line by replacing the XK140 with the XK150 and even faster XK150S.

■The Jaguar D-type wins Le Mans for the third time in a row.

■Jaguar had planned to finish a number of remaining D-type chassis as two-seater XKSS sports cars, but a serious fire at the Coventry factory destroys nine of the twenty-five cars, which had been fully or partially completed, and the project is discontinued. Amazingly, Jaguar manages to continue production of its other models almost uninterrupted in spite of the devastation at the Browns Lane site.

■The maximum speed limit for all HGVs is raised from 20mph to 30mph, some having been restricted to the lower limit under the Road Traffic Act 1930.

LOTUS ELITE

The Elite was revolutionary when it was announced in 1957. It was extremely light in weight, the body being a unitary stressed fibreglass unit. This meant that with just 75bhp from its 1,216cc Coventry Climax OHC aluminium engine it was capable of 118mph, with superb handling from its fully independent suspension and excellent acceleration of 0–60 in around 11 seconds. It was also equipped with all-round disc brakes and could return 35–40mpg. The advanced fibreglass construction was not without problems, however. When production ceased in 1963, 1,030 had been built. It cost £1,966 new.

Jaguar XKSS.

Motorway police patrolling the M1 in 1959.

1958 Britain's very first motorway, the 8-mile stretch of the M6 forming the Preston bypass, is opened, costing £4million. Drivers are warned not to picnic on the verges and could be fined £20 for driving the wrong way. U-turns were illegal but often made as there was no central barrier.

■ Britain's first motorway police are introduced on the Preston bypass (M6) using Ford Zephyr Estates and MGAs.

■ Construction work starts on the M1, originally seen as the London to Birmingham motorway, before it was planned to skirt Birmingham to the east and go further north. Technically, it is only the third motorway to be started, as the Preston bypass was part of the M6 and the Hammersmith Flyover was part of the M4.

■ Another 'golden day' for motorists, as the first parking meters are installed by Westminster City Council in Mayfair, outside the US Embassy. Parking cost 6d per hour (2.5p, or 48p in today's value) and the maximum penalty for misuse is set at £2 (£38 today). It is slightly ironic they chose a site outside the embassy, as, it could be said, most diplomats routinely ignore fines anyway.

■ The Anderson Committee adds new road signs under the Road Traffic Acts & Regulations to include signs for the new motorways, which will adopt the now familiar blue colour.

■ The six-month provisional licence is introduced.

■ The FX4 taxi appears and will become the best-known taxi in history. It remains in continuous production, with various modifications and five different engines, for thirty-nine years.

AUSTIN HEALEY SPRITE

The Sprite was the world's first volume production sports car to have unitary construction. It was planned to have retractable headlights, but cost constraints prevented this and instead the lights were in pods on the bonnet, giving rise to the nickname 'frog eye'. The engine was a mildly tuned twin-carb 948cc OHV A-series derived from the Austin 35 and Morris Minor. It delivered 43bhp, allowing 83mph, 0–60 in 20.5 seconds and around 43mpg. The first models were basic, with no boot lid and no exterior door handles. It cost £699.

■ Roads in London's suburbs see the introduction of a new 40mph speed limit.

■ The first Austin Healey Sprite is launched, becoming affectionately known as the 'frog eye'.

■ Bristol switch from the pre-war BMW derived six-cylinder engine to the 5.2-litre Chrysler V8 with the 406, the end of any link with the old BMW designs.

■ For the first time Britain produces 1 million cars in a twelve-month period.

■ Sir Leonard Lord is appointed Chairman of BMC.

■ The first traffic cones appear in Britain. They are pyramidal and made of wood and are used on the M6 construction, replacing the red oil-burning lanterns on poles used when the Preston bypass section was built.

■ Ginetta is founded by the four Walklett brothers. Their first car, the G1, was just a prototype – it is the G2 which is first made for sale. As a small company making small, lightweight sports cars it has been remarkably successful, and is still going.

■ The Ariel Leader, the first British motorcycle with flashing indicators, goes on sale.

■ Austin launch the A40 Farina.

1959 The first sections of the M1 are opened as the London to Birmingham motorway; the first stretch is the 72 miles from St Albans to Birmingham. The St Albans to Hemel Hempstead section will later be bypassed when the M1 is extended south, becoming the M10.

The first section of the M1 opened in 1959.

■ Watford Gap services opens on the M1 – the first motorway service station in Great Britain. The original plan had been for Watford Gap to service only trucks, whilst cars would use Newport Pagnell further south; however, when they open both cater for all traffic. In the early days, visiting a motorway service station is seen as a 'treat' and they even produce postcards as souvenirs and offer 'fine dining', where customers could eat whilst watching the traffic, as at Charnock Richard.

■ Double white lines in the centre of the road are introduced for the first time, indicating that they must not be crossed under any circumstances.

■ Driving examiner training is formalised and takes place at Stanmore Training School.

■ The number of cars on British roads exceeds 5 million.

■ Car ownership has reached 32 per cent of households.

■ BMC introduces the 'Mini' in both Morris and Austin forms.

■ Austin introduce the 'countryman' version of the A40 Farina, which had been launched the previous year. This was the first British 'hatchback' car.

Fortes Services on the M6 at Charnock Richard.

MORRIS MINI MINOR/AUSTIN SEVEN

The Mini, launched in 1959, revolutionised the small car market around the world and completely killed off the microcar market, which had brought some real horrors to the public. The Mini showed for the first time that a very small car can be just like a normal car except reduced in size, rather than a kiddy's pedal car scaled up to carry two or more people. The design brief had been to produce a car no more than 10ft long which could carry four adults in comfort. In addition it was a revolution in technology, with a transverse engine, rubber cone springs, a gear box contained in the engine's sump, rubber insulated sub-frames front and rear, rack and pinion steering and handling like almost nothing else on the road.

■ It was a better year for motorists as purchase tax on new cars is reduced from 60 per cent to 50 per cent.
■ Triumph introduce the Herald.
■ Lea Francis goes out of business after a long, successful run, marred by a failure to introduce a successful new model.
■ Jaguar replace the Mk1 sports saloons with the highly acclaimed Mk2, and with the potent 3.8-litre model completely revolutionising the 'get-away' vehicle market. The police respond by buying Mk2 3.8s as well.

TRIUMPH HERALD

When, towards the end of the 1950s, Standard-Triumph wanted a new small saloon car they went to car designer Giovanni Michelotti to design the bodywork, who came up with the striking 'razor-edged' look with large glass areas, giving an impressive 93 per cent all-round visibility. For complex business reasons, the Herald got a separate chassis, with all-round independent suspension and body panels, which bolted on for ease of replacement as well as variant development. At first the Standard Pennant's 948cc four-cylinder OHV engine was used. A notable feature of the Herald was an amazingly tight turning circle of just 25ft from its rack and pinion steering. The car was not an immediate success because the price, at £700, was quite high whilst the car only offered average performance – 0–60 in 31 seconds and a top speed of just 70mph from its 38bhp. But in the end the car's virtues of ease of driving, great visibility and ease of maintenance won the day and over 500,000 were produced.

Ford Anglia.

■The Ford Anglia is launched as a small family car of very conventional design, apart from the rear window, which sloped the wrong way. Contrary to rumours at the time, the rear window was not a second windscreen used because of a surfeit of these items.

■The full set of double white lines, solid and dotted, and hatched areas with both solid and dotted edges are introduced to control overtaking on major roads.

■Following the initial experience on the M6 Preston section, a decision is taken that all five police forces covering the M1 will also use Ford Zephyr Farnham-bodied estates finished in white and filled with blue flashing lights.

■A British car wins Le Mans again, although this time the baton is handed to Aston Martin with its DBR1.

■Just before the end of the decade, Bentley and Rolls-Royce launch the S2 and Silver Cloud II, saying goodbye to the smooth and very quiet straight six, and introduce the V8, which is still, with modifications, used today.

■Marcos is founded by Jem Marsh and Frank Costin. The early cars are unusual in having a plywood chassis, the result of Costin having worked on the de Havilland Mosquito.

The Swinging Sixties and the Start of the Motorway Age

The 1960s saw a dramatic decline in new business start-ups, with no new 'big names' appearing at all apart from Vanden Plas in 1960, which was really just 'badge engineering' within BMC. The other new starters were small specialist businesses, including Gordon Keeble, Warwick and Ogle, all in 1960; Piper in 1967; and McLaren in 1969.

However, some big names disappeared: Standard in 1963, Alvis in 1967, Lagonda in 1964 and Armstrong Siddeley and Allard in 1960. Several specialist manufacturers also disappeared, including Peerless in 1960, Berkeley in 1961, Turner in 1966 and Elva and Rochdale in 1968.

An indication that the car market was becoming tougher for the small players was that Gordon Keeble and Warwick closed down within a few years of starting up: Gordon Keeble in 1967 and Warwick in 1962, after just two years.

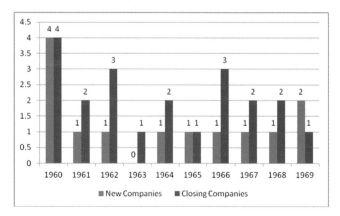

HISTORY OF STREET LIGHTING

Marginally more racy than road surfaces, street lighting has seen many changes over the years.

1405: The first reference to public lighting in Britain. The aldermen of the City of London are ordered to ensure that from dawn to dusk when the 'moon is dark', a lantern is hung outside every house along a public highway.

1461: The first technical specification for street lighting is issued by the aldermen in London, requiring the candles for the lanterns to be twelve to the pound or larger.

1599: The technical specification is upgraded to a maximum of eight candles to the pound.

1657: The aldermen of the City of London were ordered to supply public lighting where the responsibility could not be reasonably placed on individual private householders. This is the world's first example of a municipal body assuming responsibility for any part of public lighting.

1700s: During the eighteenth century, candles were increasingly being replaced by oil lamps outside private houses, for better light and less maintenance.

1807: The first gas lamps in Britain are installed in Golden Lane in London.

1812: Parliament grants a charter to the London & Westminster Gas, Light & Coke Company to provide street lighting, making it the world's first commercial gas company.

1833: The Lighting & Watching Act (1833) is passed, allowing parish councils to become lighting authorities in their own right.

1855: The Metropolis Management Act (1855) requires metropolitan boroughs to provide adequate street lighting in their areas. London boroughs thereby become, for the first time, legally responsible for street lighting.

1875: Russian Pavel Yablochkov invents the arc lamp, the light coming from the brilliant arc produced between two carbon electrodes.

1878: The first electric street lights are arc lamps installed along Holborn Viaduct and the Victoria Embankment in London as a trial. The same year Joseph Swan demonstrates the incandescent light bulb he has invented, one year ahead of Edison's 'independent invention' of the same in the US.

1879: The first permanent electric street lights are installed in Mosley Street, Newcastle upon Tyne. These are not arc lamps but Swan's incandescent lamps.

1881: The first 'high mast' lighting installation appears in front of the Bank of England, each 80ft iron trellis mast carrying one arc lamp in a clear globe. In total there are now 4,000 arc street lights in Britain.

1882: The City of London is the first local authority to light streets with incandescent bulbs when Holborn Viaduct is changed from arc lamps.

1883: Siemens conduct a trial of arc lamps on 80ft lattice poles outside the Royal Exchange in the City of London.

1884: The local authorities in Wimbledon conduct a series of experiments with incandescent lamps for street illumination. A 1-mile-long stretch of road is illuminated using 50-candle-power lamps, 100ft apart, suspended 20ft high from cables.

1892: The Private Works Act (1892) requires proper street lighting to be installed on a private road before it can be adopted as a Public Highway, a ruling which still applies today.

1900: The City of London is the first authority to introduce powers authorising street lighting to be fixed to buildings to save footpath space. Also in 1900 Cooper-Hewitt develop the first mercury discharge lamp.

1904: the first automatic gas lamplighter is introduced by the Horstmann Gear Company, removing the need for lamplighters.

1908: GEC become the first manufacturer in Britain of tungsten filament bulbs, after years of making the shorter-lived carbon filament variety.

1919: Arthur Compton of Westinghouse Electric in the US patents the first sodium discharge lamp, which will become so important in street lighting.

1926: Concrete Utilities install reinforced concrete lamp posts in Liverpool – the first in Europe.

1927: GEC introduce the first Rough Service Lamps using vibration and shock resistant tungsten wire, which offers a much extended life.

1932: Philips demonstrate the sodium bulb in Purley Way, Croydon, introducing the now familiar orange glow. The same year GEC demonstrate the rival medium-pressure mercury vapour lamp, known as the 'MA' lamp, in East Lane, Wembley.

1933: Philips starts production of AC sodium bulbs for street lighting. The same year, the first full commercial installation of medium-pressure mercury vapour lamps takes place in Watford Road, Wembley. The mercury vapour lamps give a white light, considered in many ways superior to the orange sodium 'glow', but are actually less efficient.

1935: Philips demonstrates for the first time an experimental 'MB', or high-pressure mercury lamp, although commercial applications are still two years away.

1936: Around this time there were three competing technologies: the gas lamp, the sodium lamp, and the medium-pressure mercury lamp. Gas was still being installed, the Great West Road being lit in 1936 by Rochester Gas Lamps, and Wandsworth started using gas lamps for their streets. However, Osira mercury lamps were growing in use, including in Newport, Reading, Tunbridge Wells, Lewisham, Lambeth and Norwich.

1937: High-pressure mercury lamps become commercially available for the first time from various manufacturers, including GEC, who also offer a more powerful 400-watt mercury fluorescent lamp (MAF).

1939: Fluorescent lamps appear, which are high-pressure mercury lamps within a silica envelope covered in a fluorescent coating. As war breaks out the chief form of illumination in London remains the arc lamp, and some towns like Leamington Spa were still 100 per cent gas lit.

1944: After four years the blackout regulations start to be relaxed, replaced by the so-called 'dim out'.

1945: Leamington Spa switches back on its ancient gas lighting, but decides to modernise to electric. A warmer white mercury tube is developed by BTH. Europe's first fluorescent street lighting scheme is installed in Eglington Street, Dublin.

1946: The UK's first installations of high-pressure fluorescent mercury lamps take place, firstly in Rugby High Street, then in Old Bond Street and Brompton Road in London.

1948: The City of London decides to replace all its street lights with fluorescent mercury lighting.

1951: As gas prices start to rise many authorities, such as Northampton, abandon gas for electricity, due to cost.

1953: This year sees frantic activity to update street lighting following the war. All three technologies – tungsten incandescent, sodium and mercury fluorescent – are being used, different cities going for different solutions. There are still a few new gas installations adding to the 650,000 gas lights already in use.

1954: New, more powerful and more compact mercury high-pressure fluorescent lamps are introduced.

1955: The battle of the technologies continues. GEC claim their Osram sodium lamps are still the first choice for new, large installations and make claims for cost savings and better road safety, a claim repeated by Philips for their sodium lamps a year later.

1958: Crompton-Parkinson announce an improved performance mercury lamp, with longer life and greater efficiency.

1963: The first significant technological developments for several years are demonstrated: the high-pressure sodium lamp and the mercury iodide lamp.

1964: The elevated section of the M4 between Chiswick and Langley becomes the first motorway to be illuminated, by linear sodium lanterns.

1965: The first trial installation of mercury iodide lamps takes place at Shaw in Manchester by GEC.

1966: In January, GEC install prototype high-pressure sodium lights at East Lane, Wembley. They also install the first very high mast lighting at both Severn Bridge approaches and at the Brent Cross Flyover.

1967: GEC, Philips and BLI all launch commercial high-pressure sodium lamps, the first full installation is on Southend-on-Sea ring road. The City of London starts full-scale relighting using HPS.

1968: GEC invent a form of HPS lamp which can be simply swapped over for mercury lamps without any change of control gear.

1972: The first full-scale motorway and major trunk road 'catenary' lighting is installed on the M62 and A4 in Hounslow. However, 'Spaghetti Junction' is lit by low-pressure sodium units.

1973: The urban motorway into Leeds city centre is lit by high-mast, high-pressure sodium lights. Meanwhile low-pressure sodium continues to develop, offering substantial cost savings.

1973–present: The subsequent developments have really been just ongoing refinements to existing technology, and in particular high-pressure and low-pressure sodium lamps. However, it is very likely that in the near future LED technology will play a major role in street illumination, due to its efficiency, long life, low maintenance and compact size.

Britain's first urban motorway.

Hammersmith Flyover.

1960 Traffic wardens first appear in London under the auspices of the Road Traffic Act 1960. The very first ticket was issued to Dr Thomas Crieghton, who was answering an emergency call to a West End hotel to help a heart attack victim.

■ Newport Pagnell, the second motorway service station, opens. Postcards were produced as souvenirs of visits there.

■ Jaguar acquires Daimler.

■ The 1 millionth Morris Minor comes off the production line at Cowley, one of a batch of 350 painted in a shade of lilac with white leather upholstery.

■ Under the Road Traffic Act 1960 it becomes an offence to drive, attempt to drive or be in charge of a motor vehicle on a road or other public place while under the influence of drink or drugs.

■ The first urban motorway is opened, the M63 Stretford–Eccles bypass.

■ OPEC is formed, giving the oil-producing countries more collective control over oil prices.

■ The first major high-level motorway viaduct is opened, the M63 Barton High Level Bridge.

■ Learner motorcyclists are restricted to motorcycles under 250cc.

■ This is a fertile year for small, specialist sports car companies to establish, including Gordon Keeble, Ogle and Warwick. The Gordon Keeble is unusual in having a tortoise on its badge, a slow animal on a very fast car. The story is that a tortoise wandered across a photoshoot for the launch and the irony of something so slow against something so fast was too good to miss. One hundred were made and ninety still survive. However, the price of £2,798 (£53,200 at today's prices) was too high to be sustainable.

1961 Jaguar launch the E-type, to the same sort of rapturous reception which had greeted the XK120 back in 1948.

■ There are now 10 million cars on British roads, and 350,000 casualties in total during the year.

■ Hammersmith Flyover opens at a cost of £1.3 million. It will be part of the M4, although initially it was not named as such. It is the first major two-level road construction since the war and incorporates precast post-stressed deck sections, supported on rubber bearings.

■ The Firestone Building, the iconic art deco building on the Great West Road, is illegally demolished over a weekend to much public outcry, spurring the

JAGUAR E-TYPE

No car in history has picked up as much praise for its looks. In 2008 the E-type ranked first in a *Daily Telegraph* online survey of the world's '100 most beautiful cars', and the same accolade was repeated in 2004 by *Sports Car International*. Maybe the highest praise was from Enzo Ferrari, which, on its release, called it 'the most beautiful car ever made'. Launched in 1961, it was the last Jaguar whose body design was strongly controlled by Sir William Lyons. The Series 1 was introduced with the triple carburettor 3.8-litre XK engine from the XK150. The earliest cars are actually the fastest, being capable of 149mph and 0–60 in 7.1 seconds, an amazing feat for a car costing just £2,097.

conservation movement. The stretch of the Great West Road where the Firestone building stood is called the Golden Mile because of the splendid art deco factories, such as the Hoover Building, which was saved.

■ The country's first automated multi-storey car park opens in London.

■ David Morgan of Burford in Oxfordshire claims the invention of the plastic traffic cone to replace the earlier wooden ones.

■ The MoT test is introduced by the Minister of Transport, Ernest Marples, for all cars ten years old or older and requires an annual inspection.

■ A rival claim to the Plymouth one in 1956 for the first self-service filling station is one opened in Southwark Road, London.

■ The Highway Code is revised again to include motorway regulations and driving discipline.

■ The first part of the M4 is completed: the Maidenhead bypass and Slough bypass. The Maidenhead bypass had actually been started in 1938 and the bridges mostly built, but it was put on hold because of the war. The Slough and Maidenhead bypass had been proposed in the Special Roads Act 1949.

■ In addition many bypass schemes that had been frozen in 1939 are now finally resurrected, and eventually open with bridges that are already thirty years old.

■ BMC announce the Morris 1100, which goes on sale next year.

■ BMC launch the Riley Elf and Wolseley Hornet versions of the Mini, very much with female purchasers in mind.

■ The MG Midget appears, which is, in fact just a 'badge engineered' Austin Healey Sprite Mk2.

The Hoover Building, London.

Southwark Road filling station.

107

AUSTIN/MORRIS 1100

Whilst the medium-sized mass-market family car market was dominated by conservative designs from Ford and Vauxhall, and the equally conservative Morris Oxford/Austin Cambridge range, when it came to the smaller family car, BMC broke away from the mainstream and continued at the technological 'leading edge' they had adopted with the Mini. ADO16, as it was officially known, was designed around the BMC A-series engine, but mounted transversely and driving the front wheels. Front disc brakes, not common yet on small cars, and hydrolastic suspension were advanced and the Pininfarina design gave as much interior space as the Cortina in a smaller car. Between 1962 and 1974, 2.1 million were sold.

FORD CORTINA

The medium-sized mass-market family car sector was very competitive in the 1960s, with Ford's Cortina competing against Vauxhall's Victor and Morris's Oxford. The car was designed to be simple to make and simple to maintain. The same OHV pushrod engine was used across the whole range (apart from the Lotus Cortina), differing only in capacity, with 1,197cc and 1,498cc versions available, both being enlarged versions of the engine in the Ford Anglia. The larger engine was tuned and given twin carbs to deliver 78bhp for the Cortina GT. The Mark 1 Cortina was extremely successful and nearly 1 million were sold.

■The Ford Cortina (Mk 1 as it would later become known) is introduced as a simple no-frills medium-size saloon.
■Leyland Motors acquires Standard Triumph and AEC.
■The first automatically controlled level crossing is opened at Spath near Uttoxeter.
■The Tufty Club is formed to teach road safety to young children.

1962 The 'Tiredness Kills' campaign is launched. It had been noticed that accidents on the 5 miles of the M1, both north and south, after Newport Pagnell Services were significantly less than on the 5 miles approaching in both directions, and this was attributed to the effects of tiredness.
■The Road Traffic Act 1962, sometimes known as the 'Marples Act', extends the ruling on driving under the influence of alcohol or drugs to a more general definition of 'the ability to drive properly was for the time being impaired'.

■ The AC Cobra is announced. It will have a most unexpected, profound and permanent influence on motoring in Britain.

■ Panda crossings, a forerunner of pelican crossings, are introduced – the first one at Waterloo in London – but they are not a success. They had two fundamental flaws. Firstly, the indication to the pedestrians was planned to say 'cross' or 'don't cross', but it was then realised that 'Don't Cross' would violate rights-of-way laws. Secondly, a pulsating amber light indicated to motorists that they should prepare to stop, but a flashing amber light also indicated to motorists that they could continue if the crossing were clear. In the end, pulsating and flashing were found to be too similar, with potentially fatal results.

The automatic level crossing at Spath.

■ A specific MoT Commercial Vehicle Test is introduced.

■ A valid MoT vehicle test certificate must now be produced in order to get a tax disc.

■ The Triumph Spitfire is launched as a direct competitor to the MG Midget.

■ The MGB is launched to replace the MGA. It has a monocoque construction unlike the previous car.

■ The first section of the M5 opens, the 26-mile section between Junction 4 at Lydiate Ash and the junction with the M50 in the south.

■ The Series IV Humber Super Snipe is the first British car to feature quadruple headlights.

■ The Voluntary Register of Approved Driving Instructors is approved by Parliament.

1963 The Hillman Imp is unveiled as a competitor for the Mini. It is the first car to be manufactured in Scotland since the 1931 Arrol Johnston.

HILLMAN IMP

The Hillman Imp, launched in 1963, was the Rootes Group's first new small car after the war. It was developed mainly as a Mini rival, although the approach was quite different. The Imp was powered by a lightweight aluminium 875cc engine, which was a modified Coventry Climax unit and mounted behind the rear wheels. To combat the tendency for oversteer with a rear engine design, the suspension was the subject of very careful design, being independent all round and trailing arms at the rear. The Imp was a huge risk for Rootes: quality was often suspect and sales never achieved expectations. It was withdrawn in 1976 after just 500,000 had been built and Rootes itself collapsed just two years later.

ROVER P6 2000

The P6 2000 was a complete break from the staid 'bank manager' image of Rovers, and was pitched head-to-head against the Triumph 2000 launched the same year. There were differences, though. The Triumph had a six-cylinder engine, often thought of as the requirement for the 'executive' category, whereas the Rover had only four cylinders. However, the Rover made up for this 'deficiency' by having an advanced technical specification: an overhead cam, de Dion tube rear suspension, four-wheel disc brakes inboard at the rear and removable body panels bolted onto an inner monocoque shell. It was one of the first cars to offer Denovo run-flat tyres.

Dartford Tunnel.

Thelwall Viaduct.

■The Ford Cortina is now available with a 1.5-litre engine, and a high-performance Lotus version with twin-cam engine is also launched.

■Rover introduce the 2000 P6 saloon.

■Car registrations start to include a date letter at the end, after three letters and three numbers. Not all councils change at the same time, some delaying until 1966, as they have plenty of old registrations to use up. The date letter is to change on 1 January each year.

■The Dartford Tunnel is opened. The idea for a tunnel crossing was first promoted by Kent and Essex county councils in 1929. A pilot tunnel was completed in 1938, although the Second World War meant the tunnel was not completed to full diameter and opened to traffic until 1963.

■The first pedestrianised streets are introduced in London as an experiment.

■The first section of the M2 is opened, the Medway bypass.

■The Thelwall Viaduct on the M6 opens. At 4,414ft it is the longest motorway bridge in the country at the time. Later, a second bridge will be added to allow three lanes in each direction.

■There is now an automatic driving disqualification for anyone with three driving convictions within a three-year period.

■Vauxhall launch the Viva, the first of a series of very successful small cars.

■Sir Colin Buchanan publishes his report 'Traffic in Towns', which was commissioned by the Ministry of Transport. It makes many recommendations which would influence the management of traffic in towns and cities.

■The Winchester taxi is launched by Winchester Automobiles (West End) Ltd, and has a glass-fibre body, the first London cab built from this material. But production was small and ceased in 1972.

1964 Box junctions with yellow cross-hatching first appear in London.

■The Forth Road Bridge (top right) is opened. At a total length of 8,241ft, it is the longest suspension bridge span outside the United States and the fourth longest span in the world at the time of its construction.

■BMC launch the Austin 1800 and 2200 medium-sized saloons following the same front-drive, transverse-engine approach of the Mini and 1100. They are noted for their generous internal passenger space.

■The Mini Moke, a stripped down Mini, is launched with a view to military sales. The first Mokes are extremely basic, even the front passenger seat being an optional extra.

■The elevated section of the M4, the longest road viaduct in Europe at 2 miles long, is opened. One of the major contractors was Marples, of which the Minister of Transport Ernest Marples was chairman and a major shareholder. He temporarily sold his shares in the company to avoid a conflict of interest, with an agreement to buy them back at the same price when he left office.

■The same stretch of motorway becomes the first to be illuminated.

■Thirty European countries had agreed common system of road signs in 1949. Britain finally adopts them in 1964, making 1.5 million existing road signs redundant.

■A US study suggests that having more than 80mg of alcohol per 100ml of blood sharply increases the crash risk for most drivers.

Austin-Morris 1800.

■Triumph launch their 2000 as a direct competitor to the Rover 2000.

■Following many years of crippling strikes the Rootes Group sells a controlling interest to Chrysler.

■The Clyde road tunnel opens. It had originally been approved in 1948, but construction didn't begin until 1957.

1965 The death toll on Britain's roads reaches 7,952, the highest since the wartime blackout when it peaked at 9,000.

■A 70mph blanket speed limit is introduced as a four-month experiment; the previous year an AC Cobra had been tested at 180mph on the M1. The general

Triumph 2000.

AC Cobra – the cause of the 70mph limit?

public perception is that this is not a coincidence, but this is denied by the government – and of course we believe them. A limit of 30mph is also imposed on motorways when affected by fog.

■ A new 50mph limit is introduced on certain rural trunk roads.

■ The first three-level motorway interchange is opened, the M6/A6 Fylde junction. Is this a training exercise for Spaghetti Junction?

■ Government announces its intention to introduce maximum blood alcohol levels for drivers.

■ BMC's intended merger with the Pressed Steel Company is referred to the Monopolies Commission.

■ An automatic gearbox designed by AP becomes available on the Mini, a first for such a small car.

■ Rolls-Royce announce the Silver Shadow/Bentley T, their first model without a separate chassis, greatly reducing the scope for specialist coachwork to be fitted.

■ The last councils change to using date letters in registrations, having exhausted all their old format plates.

■ The government announces the setting up of the DVLC in Swansea to administer centrally all driving and excise licences. The DVLC is to be supported by eighty-one Local Licensing Offices. It would take up until 1974 for the DVLC and all its systems to be fully operational.

■ The 'halt' sign is replaced by the 'stop' sign.

ROLLS-ROYCE SILVER SHADOW

The Silver Shadow was the first monocoque car that Rolls-Royce built, which had implications for coachbuilding. The previous Silver Clouds, with their separate chassis, were well suited to coachbuilding, but the monocoque Shadow severely limited what a coachbuilder could do. The Shadow introduced independent rear suspension, self-levelling suspension and disc brakes to the Rolls, but used the same alloy V8 that had been in the Cloud III, which produced 172bhp from its 6.2 litres. Built from 1965 to 1976 as the Shadow I, then as the Shadow II until 1980, it was the largest volume production of any Rolls-Royce model. Its list price in 1965 was £6,557, equivalent to £105,000 today.

■The driving test sight test is changed to reading a number plate with 3¹/₈in characters at a distance of 67ft.
■The Severn Bridge opens, making it Britain's first major motorway river crossing and the first motorway toll bridge.
■Flashing turn indicators become compulsory on all new cars.

1966 The give way rule at roundabouts, known as the offside rule, is formally introduced following research on roundabout safety at the Transport Research Laboratory.
■Jensen launch the FF, featuring four-wheel drive, a powerful V8 engine, bold Italian styling and the world's first production car with anti-lock brakes.
■The first four-level motorway interchange is opened, the M4/M5 Almondsbury interchange.
■The Vauxhall Viscount, a deluxe version of the Cresta, is the first mass-produced British car to have electric windows and power steering.
■British Motor Holdings is formed by merging the Jaguar Group (Jaguar, Daimler, Guy, Coventry Climax, Henry Meadows) with BMC. Sir William Lyons retires as Managing Director of Jaguar, becoming Chairman and Chief Executive as the merger is announced.
■Ford update the highly successful Cortina with the Mk2.

The Severn Bridge.

JENSEN FF

The Jensen FF was the world's first road car equipped with four-wheel drive (the Fergusson Formula system) and anti-lock braking (the Dunlop Maxaret system). The whole set up had been tested on the previous CV-8 model. Although very innovative, it suffered from two problems: a very high price and the fact it could only be right-hand drive, as the mechanical components intruded into the left-hand footwell; furthermore, the steering gear and brake servo could only be fitted on the right. This meant that most foreign markets were closed to it – great car, flawed strategy! Its appearance, however, was sensational and the normal Interceptor was quite successful.

■The plans for London's 'Ringway 1' are published, but only two sections will eventually be built – the East Cross Route from Hackney to Kidbrooke via the Blackwall Tunnel, and a section of West Cross Route known today as the Westway.
■The speed limit for public service vehicles (PSVs) is raised from 40mph to 50mph.

1967 Plans for the London Ringway 2 are published. Only a short stretch of the ringway, at first called the M11 extension and intended to be called the M15, will actually be built and this is now part of the improved North Circular.
■Rover and Alvis are acquired by the Leyland Motor Corporation.
■The national 70mph limit, introduced as an 'experiment' in 1965, is made permanent. It is not referred to as a '70mph' limit, but as 'the national limit', opening the door for future changes without major new legislation.
■Ford introduce 1,300cc and 1,600cc cross-flow engines into their Cortina range.
■The MoT test is extended to include all cars over three years old.
■The first motorway tunnel is opened, the M4 Crindau (or Brynglas) Tunnel near Newport.
■Breathalyser tests are introduced by the Labour Minister of Transport Barbara Castle – ironically, she isn't a motorist and doesn't have a licence. The limit is set at 80mg of alcohol per 100ml of breath. Refusal to provide a specimen for laboratory test becomes an offence and is taken as de facto failing the test.
■The number of cars on British roads reaches 10 million, implying just 40m of road for each motor vehicle.
■Ford UK and Ford Europe start to coordinate development and production programmes to increase common usage of components and common design approach.
■The timing of the date letter change on registrations is moved from 1 January to 1 August to boost new car sales.
■Front seat belts and their wearing become compulsory.
■Piper Cars start selling their specialised Piper GT as a kit for home completion. The Piper uses Triumph Herald front suspension and Ford rear axle and is able to take a variety of engines. It is one of the last 'kit cars' to be launched.
■Construction of Birmingham's Bull Ring 'urban motorway' begins.
■The first Tyne road tunnel opens. Having been proposed in 1937, it was approved in 1943. In 1947 the first bore was drilled to carry pedestrian traffic only.
■The second Blackwall Tunnel opens, the first having been opened in 1897.
■Rover launch the final version of the P5 with the 3.5-litre V8 engine.

M4 Crindau (Brynglas) Tunnel.

1968 Ford introduce the Escort range, including a high-performance twin-cam version.

■ Regulations are introduced concerning the minimum permissible tyre tread depth for cars. This is set at a minimum of 1mm across ¾ of the width of the tyre.

■ A tyre check, including the tread depth, is added to the MoT test.

■ The last Routemaster bus is delivered to London Transport.

■ The route for the last 48-mile section of M4 linking the Maidenhead bypass section to Swindon is finally announced, following what was known as the 'direct route'. This created some anomalies which still exist today. These include the only dual-numbered motorway junction, J8/9 (junctions 9a and 9b of the M4 aren't actually on the M4 anymore but on the A404M instead) and traffic lights on the roundabout at J8/9, which are under motorway regulations.

■ The driving test fee is increased from £1 to £1 15s.

■ The first two-level motorway viaduct is opened, the M1 Tinsley Viaduct.

■ The largest car company in British history is formed by the merger of British Motor Holdings with Leyland Motors to create British Leyland Motor Corporation.

■ Rover starts to offer their 3.5-litre Buick-derived V8 engine in the P6 body with a model called the '3005', later to be changed to the '3500'.

■ The first computerised warning signs appear on a motorway, the M4 Severn Bridge section. The London section also introduces the signs the following year.

■ The first roadside breathalyser – the Alcotest 80 'blow into the bag' arrangement – is 'type approved'.

Ford Escort.

M1 Tinsley Viaduct.

ROVER P5 V8

The V8 was the final incarnation of the very successful P5, using the lightweight alloy 3,528cc Rover V8 engine developed from the original Buick design. The engine was only lightly stressed, delivering 160bhp. Over 11,000 were sold. One of the curiosities of the P5B is that the trim of the nearside front wing stops is some 4mm short of the nearside front indicator gasket, whereas the trim on the offside front wing goes all the way to the indicator gasket. The trims themselves differ in length by less than 2mm, the wings making up the rest of the difference. Such manufacturing variances were not uncommon in cars of that era but the P5B is both consistent and noticeable in this respect.

Hogarth Flyover.

Part of the A3 Kingston bypass just before it opened in 1969.

■Britain's worst-ever level crossing accident occurs at Hixon. Eleven people are killed on the train when it hits a car transporter on the crossing.
■The Highway Code is revised and enlarged again.

1969 A separate licence category and driving test is introduced for people only wishing to drive automatics.
■The Jaguar XJ6 launched, marking a new era for Jaguar saloons and consolidating all Jaguar saloons into one model.
■The Austin Maxi, Alex Issigonis's last design, is launched. Although practical, its boxy styling, notchy gearbox, lack of power and utilitarian interior attract some criticism.
■Britain's, and possibly the world's, first mini roundabout is installed in Peterborough. It was removed in 2008.
■The Hogarth Flyover, a one-way steel structure intended as a 'temporary' relief for congestion at the Hogarth Roundabout on the A4 in London, is opened. It was planned to be there for just five years. It is still there forty-three years later!
■The first pelican crossings are installed.
■Many bypasses planned pre-war are still being completed.
■British Road Services is renamed as the National Freight Consortium.

JAGUAR XJ6

The XJ6 was a new departure for Jaguar, as it consolidated all its complex saloon range into one new model, carrying over from the previous Mark X model the engines and the independent rear suspension. At launch in 1968 two XK engines were offered: a 2.8 litre and a 4.2 litre. Power steering and leather upholstery were standard and air conditioning was an option. Another feature inherited from the Mark X was the unusual use of twin fuel tanks. In 1970 the automatic transmission offered manual gear selection on top of fully automatic to suit the sportier driver. A Daimler version was offered, and in 1972 the V12 powered model joined the range.

A Decade of Disruption and Uncertainty

The 1970s saw the lowest level of start-ups since the dawn of motoring, just eight new businesses appearing in the whole decade. In contrast twenty businesses ceased trading. The only well-known new businesses were Jensen Healey in 1972 and Caterham in 1973. A lot of well-known makes vanished, including Singer in 1970, Austin Healey in 1971, Wolseley in 1975, and Hillman, Humber, Jensen, Jensen-Healey and Sunbeam in 1976. A number of specialist makers also closed, including Ogle in 1972, Gilbern and Fairthorpe in 1973, Bond in 1974 and Piper in 1975.

Much of the decline since the 1960s was the indirect effect of 'badge engineering', whereby many old names such as Hillman, Humber, Wolseley and Riley were just cosmetically different cars from other brands. Rationalisation then led to the 'badge-engineered' ranges being reduced in scope.

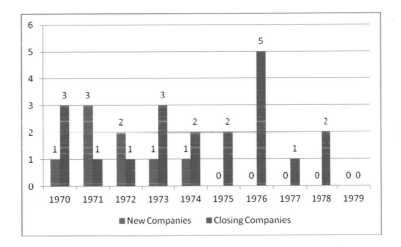

SAFETY ON OUR ROADS

One thing that is very clear from the timeline is that our roads have become much safer than they used to be. One of the standard measures of safety is the number of annual fatalities per 1,000 vehicles on the road. The earliest days were relatively safe, mainly because cars were so slow, and the vast majority of the population never even saw a car, never mind the risk of getting knocked down and killed by one. And the chance of two cars colliding was virtually zero.

Back in 1899, when Edwin Sewell and Major James Richer were thrown from their car, suffering fatal injuries, there were around 5,000 cars on the roads. So those two unfortunate deaths represented 0.4 fatalities per 1,000 cars, which was actually quite good in retrospect. But things would quickly get much worse as the number of cars increased rapidly and the number of unfortunate pedestrians coming into intimate contact with one escalated. In the early days statistics are difficult, or even impossible, to obtain. Until registration started in 1904 there was no way of knowing how many cars and other vehicles there were. Also road deaths were not reported separately from other accidents in a reliable way until the 1920s. By 1926 there were 1,715,000 motor vehicles registered and 4,886 road fatalities, giving 2.9 fatalities per 1,000 vehicles. This figure remained fairly constant until 1934, varying between 2.9 and 3.2. In 1935 the compulsory driving test was introduced. An immediate drop in fatalities was seen and by 1938 had reduced to 2.1 fatalities per 1,000 cars. Although impossible to prove, it seems likely that the driving test was largely responsible for this.

However, things were to change dramatically for the worse. The Second World War brought blackouts to the streets, and with street lights turned off and cars, where they were allowed to run at all at night, having to use extremely restricted lights, the fatality rate rose quickly. In 1939, with only part of the year affected, the rate rose to 2.6 but then leapt to around 3.8, peaking at 4.1 in 1944. Interestingly, the actual number of fatalities remained fairly constant, but the number of vehicles registered had fallen by 49 per cent since 1939. The end of hostilities, and the end of the blackout, saw a dramatic improvement in safety and by 1946 fatalities were running at around 1.5 per 1,000. Since 1946 there has been a steady improvement in safety and by 2010, with just 1,857 fatalities and 31.3 million vehicles registered, the fatality rate has fallen to just 0.06 per 1,000. In other words, relative to traffic levels, 1941 was sixty-eight times more dangerous a time to be on the roads, a sobering statistic. Unfortunately, 2011 saw a very slight increase in fatalities to 1,901, from 1,857 the year before, the first increase since 1951.

So what has given rise to a fifty-three-times improvement in safety since the 1920s, and a sixty-eight-times improvement since the worst year of 1941? There have been many factors contributing to better cars, better roads and better drivers and it is impossible to allocate proportions of the improvement to a single cause.

1970 The HGV driving test becomes compulsory for drivers of heavy goods vehicles.

■ Britain's highest motorway, the M62 section around junction 22, opens and reaches a height of 1,220ft. The M62 also features the first section of heated road surface in the country and is part of the unsigned Euro-route E20 Shannon to St Petersburg (I bet not many readers knew that). It also, uniquely, as shown in the photograph, has one section where there is a farm, Stott Hill Farm, contained within the central reservation (the farmer refused to sell his land).

■ The Register of Approved Driving Instructors comes into force and is mandatory.

■ The first stretch of motorway with four lanes in both directions is opened – the M61 Worsley Interchange.

- There are now 15 million cars on British roads.
- The first double mini roundabout is installed at Upton Cross in Dorset.
- The Range Rover is launched and creates an entirely new sector, the luxury off-road car. This sector would grow enormously over the next forty years.
- Triumph launch the Dolomite and Toledo.
- Chrysler reveal the 160/180 range at the Paris Salon to very mixed reviews. It will go on sale in the UK in 1971.

RANGE ROVER

The Range Rover, launched in 1970, created a totally new sector of the car market – the luxury 4x4 – although it wasn't originally intended as such. It was intended as a much more utilitarian 'working' vehicle whose interior, with no carpets and vinyl seats, could be hosed down! Furthermore, uniquely, the body style was devised entirely by the engineers as a temporary 'cover' to allow the chassis to be road tested. However, the board loved the shape, and so it was launched. The Range Rover had a traditional body-on-chassis construction and originally came with a 3,528cc fuel-injected Rover V8 engine, delivering 135bhp through a two-range transfer box and full permanent four-wheel drive. It also featured disc brakes all round. Over the years the Range Rover evolved from utilitarian workhorse to top-drawer luxury transport.

CHRYSLER 180

Chrysler went through a period of twelve years of badly misjudging the upper end of the market. Chrysler's Rootes division had planned a car to cover the whole spectrum from a 2-litre base Hillman through to a stretched version to replace the Humber Super Snipe. They proposed both four-cylinder and V6 engines. In the end only four-cylinder models were made, with 1.6-, 1.8- and 2-litre units. The combination of a small four-cylinder engine and a large 'luxurious' body, whilst quite a normal combination in France, never caught on in the UK or most other European markets, and sales were disappointing. But this didn't stop Chrysler making the same mistake again, only worse, with the Talbot Tagora, an even larger four-cylinder model, which replaced the 180. That was a total disaster and lasted less than two years.

TRIUMPH STAG

The Stag was a brilliant concept let down by technical issues, the main problem being that Triumph were trying to be too clever. Triumph's engineering strategy had been to create a family of engines of different capacities and numbers of cylinders around a common crankshaft. They planned engines of four, six and eight cylinders ranging from 1.5 litres to 4.0 litres. The Stag would have the V8, whilst half the engine, a slant straight four, would power cars like the Dolomite and TR7. The Stag's engine was the first to go into production. Upon launch in 1970 many problems arose with the engine: serious overheating; a mix of iron and aluminium in the engine, which required corrosion inhibitor at all times – often ignored by owners; timing chains, which stretched and failed within 20,000 miles; and cylinder heads, which warped and failed. These issues, not surprisingly, gave the car a very poor reputation for reliability. Many cars were later converted to a Rover V8 powered engine, which would have been a more sensible choice from day one.

■ Triumph launch the sensational but controversial Stag, with its notoriously unreliable engine.

1971 The Green Cross Code is introduced.
■ Zig-zag markings are added to zebra and pelican crossings and it becomes an endorsable offence to park or overtake within them.
■ Jensen ceases producing the revolutionary FF but continues with the Interceptor.
■ The last Morris Minors are produced.
■ Jaguar make a new V12 engine available in the E-type, XJS and Daimler models. It is Britain's first post-war V12.
■ The Morris Marina is launched, giving a new definition to 'conservative' technology – it is little more than a bigger Morris Minor under the skin.
■ Aston Martin is facing financial difficulties. David Brown sells the company to financiers, but the DBS stays in production.
■ The final sections of M4 in England are completed.
■ The first section of the M3 opens. Originally conceived as the London to Basingstoke motorway, the road is built to relieve traffic on the A30 and A33 – the congested single-carriageway trunk roads that previously carried the traffic. Later it will be extended to Southampton, presumably because they discover nobody actually wants to go to Basingstoke.

Graveley Hill Interchange (Spaghetti Junction).

MORRIS MARINA

The Marina has gained an ill-deserved reputation as one of the worst cars of all time. Well, actually, it's not ill-deserved at all. The Marina was awful. In their wisdom, British Leyland had decided to use the Austin name for the more adventurous cars with front-wheel drive, transverse engines and clever suspension, and to use the Morris name for conservative, traditionally designed cars. But with the Marina they took 'conservative' to new heights! Much of the car was simply a reheated Morris Minor, a 1948 design. The Marina had been designed to use the E-series OHC BMC engines, but in the end inherited the ageing A and B series units. As if to add insult to injury, the poor Marina was lumbered with a range of typical 1970s colours, including Russet Brown, Harvest Gold, Limeflower Green, Midnight Blue, Teal Blue, Blaze Orange, Damask Red and a characteristically 1970s purple called Black Tulip. It was, however, popular with families and undemanding motorists.

■Birmingham's Bull Ring 'urban motorway' is completed. The planners are so excited by it they even produce postcards as souvenirs.
■The second Mersey tunnel, the Kingsway Tunnel, opens to traffic.

1972 1,900,000 cars are produced in Britain this year.
■16-year-olds are now restricted to mopeds not exceeding 50cc.
■Spaghetti Junction (Graveley Hill) opens, to complaints it will be dangerous, concerns which turn out to be unfounded. Rumours that some motorists who entered it in 1972 and are still trying to find their way out are exaggerated – just.
■Datsun becomes the second biggest importer of cars into Britain.
■The Lotus Esprit concept car is shown at the Turin Motor Show.
■Serious labour problems begin to beset UK car manufacturing.
■The Jensen Healey appears. Car dealer Kjell Qvale had been a dealer for Austin Healey, but with the demise of the 3000 was looking for a car to replace it. In discussion with Donald Healey and Jensen Motors the concept of their new car emerges. The car benefits from the new 2-litre twin cam 16-valve Lotus 907 engine, and it is good for 119mph.
■A prototype new taxi, called the Metrocab, is introduced. However, it fails to go into production until 1987.

The Bull Ring, Birmingham.

■Panther Westwinds Ltd is formed by Robert Jankel and starts to manufacture quite extravagant retro-style cars based on standard components from other manufacturers. They produce some extraordinary designs, ranging from the relatively sane Rio to the completely bonkers Panther 6, with six wheels and a mid-mounted 8.2-litre Cadillac engine with twin turbos. Only two of these are made, of which one still exists. The bonkers Panthers have gained some popularity as wedding cars.

■Swindon sees the first 'magic roundabout' installed, consisting of five mini round-abouts placed around one large one. Later the same year another appears in Colchester.

■Dunlop introduce the Denovo 'fail safe' run-flat system for wheels and tyres, the best run-flat system available. It becomes an optional extra first on the Rover P6 3500 in 1973.

1973 The Arab–Israeli war causes serious fuel-supply problems, with a steep rise in pump prices as OPEC becomes more influential and able to manipulate oil prices for political reasons. Supplies to Britain are severely limited and long queues form at petrol stations, with 'sold out' signs becoming commonplace. Rationing coupons are reissued as a precaution, but in the end are not used.

■In view of the petrol and diesel shortages, a blanket 50mph speed limit is imposed.

■VASCAR speed detection equipment is used by the police for the first time.

■Triumph launch the Dolomite Sprint, the first British car with four valves per cylinder and alloy wheels as standard.

■Crash helmets become compulsory for motor cyclists under the Motor Cycles (Protective Helmets) Regulations 1973.

■VAT is imposed on cars replacing the previous purchase tax.

■The physical appearance of number plates is changed for the first time since 1903. From 1 January all new vehicles are required to have reflective numbers plates, black characters on white at the front and black characters on yellow at the rear. New regulations are also introduced concerning the size, shape, font and spacing of the characters.

■Caterham Cars had been a major Lotus 7 dealer during the 1960s, and in 1973 the owner Graham Nearn purchases the rights to continue manufacturing the 7 as the Caterham 7. By the year 2012 the Lotus 7 design will have been in continuous production with only minor changes for fifty-five years.

Caterham 7.

■ Computerised driving licences are introduced and licences will no longer be issued by local authorities.
■ Multi-tone horns on private cars are banned.
■ The AA starts broadcasting its Roadwatch traffic reports on commercial radio.
■ The AA also starts its Relay service.

1974 Following the end of the oil crisis, the 70mph limit on motorways is restored, as well as the lower limits on other roads.
■ The DVLC starts centrally registering and licensing all new vehicles and begins transferring vehicles with the old-style logbook (VE60) onto the new computerised system. This exercise will not be completed until 1983.
■ Airbags start to be fitted to production cars in Britain for the first time.
■ The last E-type Jaguar leaves the Coventry factory.
■ The Aston Martin Lagonda is announced, its William Towns design looking rather like automotive origami. It has a state of the art electronic instrument panel and struggles to achieve even high single-digit mpg.

1975 The first section of the M25 between South Mimms and Potters Bar is opened. This section consists of parts of the old Ringway 3 and Ringway 4 that had been started in 1973 and then elevated to motorway status in 1975.
■ Front number plates on motorcycles are abolished.
■ Legislation is introduced making it compulsory to use headlights in conditions of seriously reduced visibility.
■ Hand turn signals cease to be part of the driving test.
■ The York bypass is opened by the Archbishop of York.
■ Rolls-Royce launch the controversial Camargue.
■ The British Leyland Motor Corporation is nationalised following years of industrial relations and money problems, and with a £200 million cash injection becomes British Leyland, or simply BL.
■ Jaguar announce the XJS to 'replace' the iconic E-type.
■ Lotus start production of the Esprit and also underline a move upmarket with the four-seater front engine Eclat.
■ British Leyland launch the controversial 'wedge-shaped' Princess, to mixed reviews. It is the first British car to have windscreen wipers which park hidden away.
■ Britain's worst ever road crash occurs at Dibbles Bridge near Grassington in North Yorkshire when a coach crashes and falls off a bridge, killing thirty-two people.

ROLLS-ROYCE CAMARGUE

The Camargue was an exclusive hand-built car based on the Silver Shadow floorpan with a Mulliner Park Ward coach-built two-door body, costing £29,250, equivalent to £203,000 in today's money. At launch it was the most expensive car in the world, but its looks have always been controversial. It was the first car in the world with fully automatic split-level air conditioning and the first Rolls-Royce fully designed using metric dimensions. It was powered by the same 6.75-litre V8 engine as the Silver Shadow, though in slightly more powerful form. During the car's eleven-year production run, 530 Camargues were built.

JAGUAR XJS

The XJS was launched as a replacement for the E-type, although many thought it a mere 'grand tourer' rather than a sports car. It was based on the XJ6 platform, but allied initially to just the 5.3-litre V12 engine. This gave splendid performance – 143mph and 0–60 in 7.6 seconds – and the cachet of a V12, at the time the territory of exotic Italian supercars like Lamborghini and Ferrari. The timing was not good for the XJS. The large V12 was launched in the wake of an oil crisis and its design attracted some criticism, especially the 'buttresses' behind the windows. Its appeal was widened considerably with the launch of the 3.6-litre six and with the more attractive open 'roadster'.

1976 The unique 2-mile-long M275 near Portsmouth opens. It was originally intended to have a junction partway along, but this had to be abandoned when planners discovered there had to be a minimum distance of 1.25 miles between junctions – the M275 simply wasn't long enough! It is also unique in that it is not managed by the Highways Agency, but by the local authority, Portsmouth City Council, and has no hard shoulders. A motorway in name at least.

■ Rover launch the 3500 SD1.

■ The Vauxhall Chevette, General Motors' first fully global car known as the 'T Car', appears in the UK as a two-door or four-door saloon.

■ The first section of the M42 opens between Birmingham International Airport and the M6.

LEYLAND PRINCESS

The Princess, originally launched as the 18-22 Series, inherited the transverse engine/front-wheel drive configuration from the 1800/2200 BMC ADO17 range, still a novel layout at the time for full-sized family cars. This layout gave the Princess an advantage in terms of interior space, although the wedge styling was controversial at the time. Princess sales, although strong for the 1976 model year, tailed off more quickly than forecast, primarily because of quality and reliability issues. Also, by 1977 many of its competitors had gained a versatile fifth door, which the Princess lacked, and the full-size family car sector fell victim to a poor economic climate, further compounded by the OPEC oil crisis of the day. Total production amounted to 224,942 units.

1977 South African Michael Edwards takes over as the boss at BL.

■A 'moped' for licence, tax and insurance purposes is now to be defined as a small motorcycle with a maximum speed of 50mph. Anything that can go faster is no longer a moped and cannot be ridden by a 16-year-old.

■The MoT test is extended to include windscreen washers, wipers, indicators, spotlights, horn, exhaust and body structures.

■The Rover 3500 SD1 wins the European Car of the Year award.

■Ford introduce the Fiesta, their first front-drive small family car.

ROVER SD1 3500

In 1971 Rover started developing a new car to replace both the Rover P6 and the Triumph 2000/2500. The car was designed for simplicity of manufacture and reverted to a live rear axle after the P6's de Dion setup. The plan had been to use the 2.2-litre four-cylinder engine, then revised to the Triumph 'six', but the fairly mundane chassis was 'rescued' by the adoption of the 3.5-litre Buick-derived V8 engine. A year later SOHC 2.3-litre and 2.6-litre sixes followed, and eventually a 2-litre four. It was unusual for a luxury car in having a hatchback. Unfortunately poor construction quality marred what was seen as technically a good vehicle.

FORD FIESTA

When launched in January 1977, the Fiesta was Ford's first front-wheel drive car sold in Britain, and also only the second hatchback 'mini' car to be built in the UK, coming one year after the Vauxhall Chevette. The basic model had a 950cc Ford BC-series engine and sold for £1,856. Engine options included a 1.1-litre and 1.3-litre OHV unit. Prior to launch several names were shortlisted, including Amigo, Bambi, Bebe, Bravo, Bolero, Cherie, Tempo, Chico, Fiesta, Forito, Metro, Pony and Sierra. Despite more board votes for Bravo, Henry Ford II personally overruled them and named the car Fiesta. One million were sold by January 1979.

1978 The Highway Code is revised again.
■ It will become mandatory to fit rear fog lamps to new cars from next year.
■ The national speed limit on ordinary roads is set at 60mph and the limit of 70mph on motorways and dual carriageways is made permanent.
■ BL starts to shows signs of recovery, with fewer damaging strikes.

1979 Rolls-Royce is sold to Vickers for £38 million.
■ Rover announce that they will start a collaboration with Honda to develop models jointly for the British and European markets.
■ Britain's longest uninterrupted (no junctions) stretch of motorway is opened, the 15.2-mile (24.3km) stretch of the M11 between junctions 8 and 9. Missing one of these junctions became recognised as the worst navigational mistake that can be made in Britain.

More Regulation and Change

The 1980s continued the low level of start-ups seen in the 1970s, although there was a small net gain of five manufacturers over the decade; however, nearly all the new businesses were small, such as a temporarily revived Lea Francis and Jensen. Two memorable start-ups were De Lorean and Sinclair, both memorable for quite different, and far from auspicious, reasons.

The casualties of the 1980s included two very big names: Morris in 1983 and Triumph in 1984, as well as Vanden Plas in 1980. Neither De Lorean nor Sinclair survived the decade, going under in 1982 and 1985 respectively.

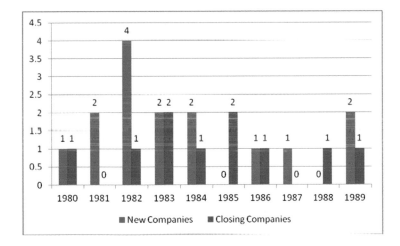

PAYING FOR OUR ROADS

Nobody enjoys paying for roads, but when we do we would at least like to think all the road 'taxes' are actually spent on roads, but this has not been the case since 1927. The way roads are paid for has changed considerably over time.

1100s: Until the thirteenth century, roads were not repaired in a systematic way, but just on an ad hoc basis as the local landowner saw fit.

1216–72: In the reign of Henry III the first organised system for road repairs started. So-called 'grants of pavage' were made to burgesses, bailiffs and mayors of English towns, permitting them to impose tolls on the movement of goods in and out in order to pay for the repair and 'paving' of streets. However, there was no proper regulation at all and inevitably corruption crept in – for example tolls being collected but no repairs carried out.

1272–1307: During his reign Edward I was fairly generous with special tolls for pavage, although pavage grants were not common before 1300.

1201–1400: Throughout the thirteenth and fourteenth centuries these 'grants of pavage' increased dramatically in number, particularly during the reign of Edward II, and were also extended to include the maintenance of roads between towns. These were granted by letters patent from the king and were for a finite period.

1555: Up to this point the responsibility, even under the grants of pavage, lay very much with the local landowners, and road repairs were very variable. The Highways Act 1555 was the first major change, marking the first state control of the road system. Every adult inhabitant of each parish was obliged to work for four consecutive days each year on road maintenance, providing their own tools, carts and horses. The work was overseen by an unpaid, locally appointed Surveyor of Highways. Rich people could 'buy off' poorer people to do their stint, however.

1563: An amendment to the Act increased the labour for roads and by 1654 there was some provision for paid labour provided centrally by the government, but the rapid increase in traffic meant there was no improvement in the roads. Legislation was introduced to set a minimum width for cartwheels of 16in, but whilst it reduced rutting, the broader wheels did not consolidate the surface as before.

1637: The first direct tax on vehicles to pay for roads appeared in 1637 when hackney cabs were required to be licensed to help maintain London's roads.

1663: The next big change came with the turnpikes, whereby travellers of all sorts paid varying tolls to pay for the maintenance of a specific stretch of road. The first turnpike appeared in 1663 on a section of the Great North Road. Toll houses, toll gates and toll collectors appeared to collect and administer the charges. The early turnpikes were overseen by local Justices of the Peace.

1706: An Act of Parliament was passed placing the management of the turnpikes in the hands of a group of appointed trustees. The first trustee-managed turnpike was a section of the London–Coventry–Chester Road.

1747: All vehicles pulled by two or more horses had to be licensed.

1790s: The 1790s saw a peak in new turnpikes being set up, at around fifty per year.

1822: A series of General Turnpike Acts (1744, 1766, 1773 1822) introduced a number of improvements to turnpikes, including compulsory milestones, parish boundary markers and distance/direction signs to major towns.

1830s: From the 1830s the development of railways led to a reduction in the use of roads for long-distance carriage of goods and people, and the last turnpike trusts were set up in 1835 and 1836.

1835: The Highways Act 1835 set up groups of parishes to look after roads, but it was not a success.

1861: The Locomotive Act 1861 required coaches and steam vehicles to purchase a licence, but these were only valid in the county of purchase, so travelling through different counties required multiple licences, although this system was not well administered.

1878: The Highways and Locomotives Amendment Act 1878 set up Highway Authorities and active disbandment of the turnpike trusts started.

1888: New duties were introduced, locomotives paying £5 and carts and carriages paying 5s per wheel.

1889: The newly formed county councils, created under the Local Government Act 1888, took over responsibility for main roads, and then in 1894 district councils accepted responsibility for local roads. Road maintenance was now paid for entirely through local rates.

1895: The very last toll gate – on the London–Holyhead Road in Anglesey – closed in 1895, marking the end of tolls paying for road maintenance until the M6 toll road opened in 2004.

1909: The Finance Act 1909–01 announced the creation of a vehicle tax based on the nominal horsepower of a car, which remained unchanged until 1949. The Act also stated that all revenue from the tax will go into a 'ring-fenced' Road Fund which will only be spent on roads. The tax is set at £2 10s for cars up to 6.5hp, rising to £42 for 60hp vehicles.

1909: In 1909 central government starts to give grants to local authorities for road maintenance from the Road Fund and for the first time central tax revenue as well as local taxes supported the roads. The government says roads are to be self-financing.

1927: The first hint of removing the 'ring fence' on car tax came when the Chancellor of the Exchequer, Winston Churchill, withdrew the entire £12 million in the fund and put it into the general national coffers – the Road Fund continued in name at least.

1920: The Ministry of Transport was set up, allowing better supervision and control of road construction and maintenance.

1930: County councils accepted responsibility for all roads.

1936: Roads designated as 'trunk roads', or major roads joining towns and cities, now came under the direct control and financial responsibility of central government.

1937: The Road Fund, which by now was empty anyway, was wound up, removing the final pretence that car tax is only spent on roads.

1938: The car tax is changed from discrete categories to a uniform £1 25s per hp.

1939: The licence disc started to say 'Mechanically Propelled Vehicle Licence' rather than 'Road Fund Licence', reflecting the reality of the dead Road Fund.

1948: The car tax is simplified to a flat £10 per vehicle.

1999: A reduced tax of £100 is introduced for cars of less than 1,100cc, the tax on larger-engined cars being set at £155.

2003: London introduces the congestion charge, ostensibly to help fund road investment in the capital.

2005: A new system of graduated car tax is introduced based on CO_2 emissions.

2009: The CO_2 bands are reclassified.

2012: Major changes in the tax system are made. A special higher rate of tax is paid for the first year of a new car before it reverts to the standard rates, and cars emitting less than 100g of CO_2 per km will pay no tax at all.

1980 Ford announce a front-wheel-drive Escort Mk3 to replace the old rear-drive model.

■ There are bitter strikes at BL and chairman Sir John Edwardes warns the workforce to 'return to work or lose your jobs'. It is the bleakest time for the British car industry.

■ Daimler-Jaguar gets John Egan as its new chairman. He expresses a commitment to rebuilding pride in the quality of design and production lost since BL days.

■ BL launch the Metro.

■ The second Dartford Tunnel is opened after eight years of construction, at a cost of £45 million. The Dartford Tunnels, technically not 'motorway', represent the only break in the M25.

■ The Parliamentary Advisory Committee on Transport Safety (PACTS) is created.

■ Rolls-Royce launch the Silver Spirit to replace the Shadow. It is the first Rolls-Royce on which the Spirit of Ecstacy is retractable, not for safety but to prevent theft.

FORD ESCORT

The third generation of Escort shared little except its name with its forebears. Whereas the Mark II had been a simple reskin of the 1968 original, the Mark III was a wheels-up design with front-wheel drive and a hatchback body. Also, apart from the base 1.1 litre, the 1.3- and 1.6-litre variants offered OHC and a sophisticated valve arrangement with hemispherical combustion chambers. As with most Fords, the Escort came in a number of trims: Popular, L, GL, Ghia and XR3. The iconic XR3, designed to go head-to-head with the Golf GTi, featured a tuned 1.6-litre engine, which evolved into the XR3i with fuel injection, then the RS1600i and finally the 132bhp turbocharged RS Turbo. There was also a diesel version with just 54bhp, which struggled to reach 90mph. Sales in the UK increased steadily and by 1982 it had overtaken the ageing Cortina as the nation's best-selling car.

METRO

The Metro was planned to supplement not replace the Mini, although the design did include some Mini underpinnings, including the 998cc and 1,275cc A-series engines, much of the front-wheel-drive train and the suspension sub-frames. The Metro used the Hydragas suspension from the Allegro. Like the Mini, the Metro offered exceptional internal space for its overall size. The name Metro was chosen by a ballot of BL employees from a choice of Match, Maestro or Metro. Of special note was the MG Metro Turbo, rather temperamental but with exceptional performance, reaching 115mph and 0–60 in 8.9 seconds. The Metro proved very popular and was the best-selling small car until the Ford Fiesta came along, selling around 1 million over ten years.

1981 Minimum driving age for disabled car drivers is reduced to 16.

■The Humber Bridge is opened. Originally proposed in 1930, the plan was revised in 1955 but construction did not begin until 1972. With a central span of 1,460m it would be the longest single-span suspension bridge in the world for the next sixteen years.

■Citizen Band Radio (CB), an import from the US, is legalised.

■The De Lorean car is launched by John De Lorean. Powered by a Douvrin PRV V6 engine, it has a shiny stainless-steel body, but the car is seen as overpriced and there are serious quality issues. More seriously, however, the company itself, and John De Lorean in particular, are caught up in a financial scandal with accusations of fraud. The company has a very short life.

■Legislation is invoked requiring all new cars to be fitted with seat belts.

■The Transport Act 1981 introduces evidential breath testing, with the legal limit being set at 35mg of alcohol per 100ml of breath, equivalent to 80mg in the bloodstream. It is not implemented until 1983.

The Humber Bridge in Yorkshire.

1982 Speed cameras are first used in trials by the British police, but could not yet be used for convictions.

■The two-part motorcycle test is introduced.

■The system of motoring convictions is radically changed. The previous system of 'totting up' offences, all with equal weight, is replaced by a 'points' system, with the number of points reflecting the seriousness of the offence. Incurring 12 points within three years will lead to disqualification (at the court's discretion).

■Total British car production falls to 888,000.

■Colin Chapman, the founder of Lotus Cars, dies suddenly aged 54.

■De Lorean goes into receivership after a few months, having built just 8,563 DMC-12s. The company is embroiled in financial scandals.

■British Leyland Cars Ltd is renamed Austin Rover.

■Aston Martin gains a Royal Warrant, although Prince Charles has been a loyal Aston Martin driver since the 1970s.

■The National Freight Consortium is sold to the employees under Margaret Thatcher's privatisation initiative. In 1989 it will be listed on the London Stock Exchange as NFC PLC.

1983 There are now 20 million cars on British roads, but the total number of casualties falls to 309,000.

■Seat belt wearing becomes compulsory for front-seat passengers.

■ Learner motorcyclists, regardless of age, are to be restricted to machines of 125cc or less.

■ The first regulations governing speed humps are introduced.

■ The MoT test for taxis and vehicles with more than eight passenger seats is now required at just 1 year old.

■ The suffix date letters for registrations are now exhausted. It is decided to introduce a simple swap from 'three letters, three numbers plus date letter' to 'date letter, three numbers and three letters'. The new format will last up until 2001.

■ Q registration plates are introduced for vehicles of indeterminate age, such as kit cars or rebuilds using new components.

■ Evidential breath testing is put into practice. The Lion Intoximeter 3000 gains type approval – the machine used at the police station to provide printouts as evidence for use in courts.

■ This year also sees the introduction of the High Risk Offenders Scheme, intended to manage convicted drink-drivers who may have an alcohol problem. Drivers who fall in this category must now satisfy the DVLA that they have overcome an alcohol problem before they will be issued with a driving licence, which involves attending a DVLA medical and providing a blood sample.

1984 25.5 million full or provisional licences are in circulation, which means half the population is driving.

■ Lorries and trailers are to be fitted with spray-reducing devices by law.

■ This year marks the final use of the Morris name on cars.

■ The name Triumph disappears as the Acclaim ceases production.

■ Austin Rover launch the Rover 200 and the Montego.

■ Jaguar is privatised through a stock market float.

MONTEGO

The Montego was a car that took a while to be loved. It was the replacement for the awful Marina, so had everything going for it. After all, it couldn't be worse! It was competing against the Sierra from Ford and the Cavalier from Vauxhall. At launch it came in two guises: Austin and MG. Originally it was to come in both saloon and five-door hatchback, but the hatchback became the Maestro, which was launched first. The MG variant was a potent machine, offering 126mph and 0–60 in 7.3 seconds, the fastest MG ever. The estate version of the base model proved particularly popular.

MG METRO 6R4

Sometimes a car appears which can only be described as bonkers – the MG 6R4 being one such vehicle. Although it was called a Metro, in reality the only things it shared with its humble sister was the name and a vaguely superficial likeness if stared at through half-closed eyes. It was mid-engined with a 2,991cc V6 24-valve unit developed from the Rover V8 and had permanent four-wheel drive. It came in two guises: the tame shopping runabout with a measly 250bhp, which was sold to the public for £40,000, and the totally bonkers 'homologation' version with 410bhp, or around 1000bhp/ton. The latter had the distinction at the time of being the fastest accelerating car ever to feature in a published road test, achieving 0–60 in under 3 seconds.

■ BL launch the totally bonkers MG 6R4 as a rally car, but must sell some to gain homologation.
■ The Road Traffic Regulation Act 1984 exempts emergency vehicles from speed limits. Before, it had, technically, been a matter of 'turning a blind eye'.

1985 Transport Act 1985 deregulates all bus services apart from London and Northern Ireland, leading to a rapid development of private bus companies, often with fierce local competition on the best routes, initially.
■ The first car phones are introduced in Britain.
■ The world's first heated windscreens, the Quickclear, appear on Ford Scorpio/Granada.
■ Tachographs first become mandatory for certain classes of goods vehicles.
■ Sir William Lyons, the man behind the growth of Jaguar, and personally behind many of their iconic models, dies just as the reputation for Jaguar quality and value that he built up starts to return.
■ By 1985 the centralisation of all licensing at the DVLC, and the appointment of 3,000 post offices to handle applications, enables the number of local licensing offices to be reduced to fifty three from eighty-one.
■ On 5 April there is 40 miles of stationary traffic on the M1 north of junction 16, laying claim to Britain's worst congestion (see also 1987).

1986 The M25 is finally completed and at 120 miles it is the longest ring road in the world. Its popularity was grossly underestimated at the planning stage and it quickly becomes infamous for traffic jams, becoming nicknamed the country's largest car park.

Chalfont Viaduct before the M25.

The M25 passing under Chalfont Viaduct – dimensions perfect!

■ One of the last sections of the M25 to open, the 13 miles from Poyle J14 to Maple Cross, includes the section under the Chalfont (Misbourne) Viaduct. Amazingly, the railway engineers in 1901 judged the arch widths exactly right – what foresight!

■ Nissan opens a large new plant in Sunderland, which will become the largest car factory in Britain.

■ Austin Rover becomes simply the Rover Group, with just the Rover and MG brands being retained.

■ The first 'eye in the sky' takes to the air. London's Capital Radio is the first to utilise an aeroplane to monitor traffic and give live broadcasts about the twenty-one worst trouble spots around the capital.

■ 1986 is the European Year of Road Safety.

■ Fixed penalties are introduced for minor motoring offences, with fixed fines replacing penalty points and court appearances.

■ Unleaded petrol goes on sale in a bid to reduce lead pollution.

■ The Rover 800 is launched, the offspring of a collaboration between Rover and Honda.

1987 All new cars now must have rear seat belts fitted on the production line.

■ Zig-zag lines appear at pelican crossings as well as zebra crossings, indicating that parking or overtaking within the zig-zag zone is an endorsable offence.

■ The Channel Tunnel is finally started, a century after the first attempt was made.

ROVER 800

Launched in 1986, the 800 was the result of collaboration between Rover and Honda and was a replacement for the SD1. The Honda Legacy and Rover 800 shared many components, although the Rover lost out badly in terms of quality and reliability, a reflection on the situation in the British car industry at the time. At launch there were two versions: the 820 with a 2-litre 16-valve development of BL's O-series engine, and the 825 with a Honda-designed 2.5-litre V6. A fastback version followed the saloon in 1988. In 1990 a diesel version was added with a 2,498cc VM Motori engine, a development of that used in the Range Rover Turbo D.

■Ford acquires 75 per cent of Aston Martin Lagonda.

■On the M61 a diesel tanker crashes into stationary traffic near Preston, killing twelve people.

■On 17 April on the M6 between Charnock Richard and Carnforth there is a traffic jam involving over 200,000 people and over 50,000 vehicles. This competes with congestion on 5 April 1985 for the claim to be the worst congestion ever in Britain.

1988 All coaches first used since 1974 must have 70mph speed limiters fitted by 1992.

■British Aerospace buys the Rover Group.

■All new cars must be able to run on unleaded fuel.

■Britain's narrowest stretch of motorway, the 7.3m-wide single carriageway, A601(M), is opened as part of the Lancaster M6/Carnforth Link Road complex.

■The longest completely stationary queue of traffic ever in Britain is reported on the M25, measured at 22 miles.

■The Saltash Tunnel opens on the A38 on the approach to the Saltash Bridge on the Cornwall/Devon border. It is Britain's first road tunnel with 'tidal' flow lane changes.

1989 Ford acquire Jaguar with a promise to build on the unique identity and value of the brand. Within a few years Ford will have rebuilt Jaguar's quality and reliability reputation.

LAND ROVER DISCOVERY

The Discovery, launched in 1989, was based on the Range Rover chassis but aimed at a lower price point to compete against Japanese offerings. The Conran-designed interior received much acclaim, the brief being to design a 'lifestyle accessory', ignoring contemporary design practices. The Discovery was available with either a 2.5-litre 200TDi or a 3.5-litre V8 petrol engine. In the first year only a three-door was available, the five-door arriving the following year. A 2-litre 'tax beating' petrol version was short-lived, being under-powered, and in any case the tax laws changed. All of them had permanent four-wheel drive, two-range transfer boxes and a locking third central differential, superior to the twin differential setup on many rivals.

The large Honda factory in Swindon.

■The Land Rover Discovery is launched.

■Children travelling in cars must now wear seat belts or approved restraints where these have been fitted.

■A tougher accompanied learner's test for motorcyclists is introduced.

■The FX4 taxi is revised to create the Fairway, including a fully wheelchair-accessible interior.

■Wheel clamping makes its first appearance in Britain in the capital.

■Honda announces plans to expand significantly in Swindon.

■The DVLA extends its traditional area of business to embrace the sale of unissued registration marks. The more valuable and prestigious plates are to be sold at auction four or five times a year. Less valuable ones are to be sold through telesales (and later on the Internet) on a first come first served basis.

■The M42 is completed with the opening of the link to the M5.

Can the Roads Cope with the Traffic?

The 1990s saw fourteen start-ups in the industry, of which the most notable were the three supercar manufacturers: McLaren in 1993, Ascari in 1995 and Noble in 1998. All the others were very small operations. In terms of casualties the revived Jensen disappeared in 1992 and the specialist Panther closed its doors in the same year. The low number of companies closing is mainly a reflection of how few companies actually still existed.

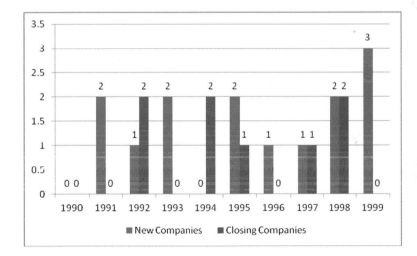

1990 The first fully coordinated motorway police force is created covering Staffordshire, West Midlands and West Mercia police. It utilises forty-six patrol cars operating out of six bases.

■ The rule which banned the restoration of old registrations to their original vehicle is relaxed and is allowed on a 'non-transferability' basis; that is the registration may be transferred back but never transferred ever again.

■ The first pilot scheme of Red Routes is started in North and East London. This scheme bans any stopping on the vital bus routes.

■ The Driving Standards Agency is created by the Ministry of Transport.

■ New regulations require learner drivers to be accompanied by someone over 21 who has held a full licence for at least three years.

■ Compulsory Basic Training (CBT) is introduced for motorcyclists.

■ Learner motorcyclists are prohibited from carrying pillion passengers.

1991 For the first time legislation is introduced to allow convictions for speeding based solely on speed cameras.

■ The Road Traffic Act 1991 provides for the decriminalisation of parking offences committed within controlled parking zones. Generally speaking these are areas with yellow lines. Parking on red routes or zig-zag areas leading up to pedestrian crossing are still classified as criminal offences.

■ From now on all rear-seat passengers must wear belts where these are fitted.

■ New 20mph zones are introduced in residential areas.

■ Speed limiters on buses and coaches are to be set at 65mph and on HGVs at 56mph.

■ White chevron markings appear on motorways to warn about separation distance.

■ The Dartford (Queen Elizabeth) Bridge is opened after three years of construction at a cost of £86 million. It is designed to relieve the pressure on the two tunnels.

■ Petrol prices soar because of the Gulf War.

■ The MoT test is extended to include emissions, anti-lock brakes and rear seat belts.

■ The M40 is opened, joining the A40 out of London to the M42 around Birmingham.

■ A new offence of causing death by driving while under the influence of alcohol or drugs is introduced, with a sentence on conviction of up to 5 years in prison.

Dartford Bridge.

■ Drink driving rehabilitation courses are introduced. Attending the course can reduce disqualification time by up to 25 per cent and can help reduce insurance premiums.

■ There is a serious crash on the M4 motorway near Hungerford involving fifty-one vehicles. Ten die in the pile-up caused by a driver falling asleep at the wheel.

■ Ariel Motors Ltd is founded, making the sensational Atom. The car is the result of a university design exercise by an undergraduate.

1992 Permanently sited speed cameras appear for the first time.

■ Britain's shortest motorway is opened, the 300m-long A635(M), part of the Mancunian Way in Manchester.

■ Jaguar launch the XJ220.

■ The 'Cones Hotline' is introduced for members of the public to complain about unnecessary cones. But has anyone ever called it?

■ All new goods vehicles over 7.5 tons are to be fitted with 60mph speed governors.

■ The minimum legal tyre tread depth is increased to 1.5mm.

■ Catalytic converters are to be fitted to all new cars.

■ Toyota open a large new plant near Derby.

■ The Association of Wheel Clamping Companies is founded.

JAGUAR XJ220

Manufactured by Tom Walkinshaw Racing, the XJ220 held the record for the fastest ever production car, at 217mph. The original concept had a quad-cam 6.2-litre V12 version of Jaguar's existing engine, with four-wheel drive by FF Developments. The concept was never intended for production, but overwhelming demand and enthusiasm led to a change of heart and Walkinshaw was asked to convert the concept into a production car. When it came to production Walkinshaw decided the V12 was too old and cumbersome, deciding instead on the much more powerful twin turbocharged 3.5-litre V6 as used in the Group C Jaguar XJR-10/11 racers, which delivered 542bhp at 7,000rpm. However, the production car was seen by some as inferior, as it 'only' had a V6 not a V12, even though the V6 was a vastly better engine; furthermore, the car came out just at the time of an economic crash, which led many people who had placed a non-refundable £50,000 deposit to try to pull out of their commitment. They couldn't and this tarnished the car unfairly. It is now seen as the sensational supercar that it was.

1993 The Highway Code is revised – again.

■The first trials are undertaken of puffin crossings with a red/green flashing man, sensors to check the crossing is clear of pedestrians and signs both opposite and on the same side so pedestrians can see the sign and the traffic at the same time.

■The MoT test is further extended to include many smaller items such as rear fog lights, registration plates and mirrors.

■Following the pilot scheme in 1990 Red Routes are introduced across the London.

■The Aston Martin DB7 is launched.

■Ford announce a greatly improved version of the Jaguar XJ6.

■The sensational McLaren F1 is finally released for sale.

ASTON MARTIN DB7

Some critics dismiss the DB7 as a fancy and expensive Jaguar XJS – it's true that the platform was based on the XJS platform and that the engine was a derivative of the straight six Jaguar unit, albeit a supercharged one delivering 335bhp and 361ft-lb of torque. The DB7 was the only Aston Martin ever to be fully built from steel, other Astons before and since have had aluminium bodies on steel chassis, whilst the very latest models feature aluminium monocoque, like the latest Jaguars. The family link between Aston Martin and Jaguar arose from their shared ownership by Ford between 1988 and 2007.

MCLAREN F1

When launched in 1993 the F1 took over the crown from the Jaguar XJ220 as the fastest car in the world. Capable of 243mph, it could achieve 0–60 in 3.2 seconds, 0–100 in 6.3 seconds and 0–150 in 12.8 seconds, as well as being able go from 30–225 using only sixth gear. But it did cost £500,000! McLaren decided on a naturally aspirated engine rather than the use of turbos, and a BMW engine was chosen – a 6,064cc quad-cam, 48-valve, dry sump V12 unit delivering 618bhp. The body was mould breaking, being the first production car with a carbon-fibre monocoque accommodating three seats, with the driver in the middle. Production began in 1992 and ended in 1998 after 106 had been made.

FORD MONDEO

The Mondeo, launched in January 1993, represented an enormous investment for Ford; in fact, it was one of the most expensive new car programs of all time, replacing the Sierra to become a truly global model. The floor plan was designed for extreme flexibility in terms of drive train, front-wheel drive was used for the first time on a medium-sized Ford and sophisticated suspension and front and rear sub-frames gave excellent handling, ride and refinement. In Britain three versions of the 16-valve Zetec engine were offered: 1.6 litre 90bhp, 1.8 litre 115bhp and 2.0 litre 136bhp, as well as a 1.8 turbo diesel. Mainly for overseas markets, a 2.5-litre V6 was also available. The Mondeo was a success and secured the future of Ford in Europe.

■The Ford Mondeo is launched as Ford's principal mid-sized car, both in Britain and Europe, and in the US, where different names are used.
■Sir David Brown, former owner and saviour of Aston Martin, dies aged 89.
■In November, a minibus carrying fourteen children and their teacher crashes into the back of a motorway service vehicle on the M40 near Warwick. Ten children and the teacher die at the scene, and two more die later in hospital. The minibus was not fitted with seat belts, as was required by law.

1994 The Channel Tunnel is completed, which is designed to carry 12,000 vehicles per day. It has cost £9 billion.
■BMW buys Rover Cars from British Aerospace.
■Buses and coaches are to be limited to 65mph and all HGVs to 56mph.
■The MoT test is extended to include diesel emissions, as diesel cars take an increasing share of the market.
■Ford acquires the remaining 25 per cent of Aston Martin Lagonda to take full ownership.
■This year marks the end of the line for the Maestro, Montego and Metro/Rover 100 series. The final legacy of BL fades away.

The Channel Tunnel, linking the UK to France.

1995 Variable mandatory speed limits are introduced on the M25, replacing advisory speeds controlled by the MIDAS system. Initially they are between J10 and J15, but are extended to J16 in 2002. The mandatory limits are enforced by speed cameras.

MG MGF

The MGF launched in 1995 was the first all new car to carry the MG name since the MGB. The MGF was produced until 2005, but Nanjing Automobile in China – the company's new owners – resumed production. The MGF was mid-engined, powered by VVC 16-valve version of the 1.8-litre K-series unit delivering 143bhp. An interesting feature of the MGF was its Hydragas suspension, a system employing interconnected fluid and gas displacers, which provided a surprisingly compliant ride but which could be tuned to provide excellent handling characteristics. The MGF quickly shot to the top of the affordable sports car charts in Britain and remained there until the introduction of the MGTF in 2002.

ROVER 200

Whereas the previous Rover 200s had been based on Honda designs, the new 200 launched in 1995 was almost entirely a new Rover design. The new car was smaller than the old 200, partly because of the need to replace the ageing Metro, which was 15 years old. The 200 was launched with 1.4-litre 16-valve 104bhp, 1.6-litre 16-valve 109bhp and 2.0-litre 85bhp turbo diesel engines. Later, 1.1-litre and 1.8-litre variants were added. At first, the third-generation 200 was a good seller, being Britain's seventh-best seller between 1996 and 1998, but by 2001 it had slipped out of the top ten altogether.

■ The Road Traffic Act (New Drivers) 1995 introduces a two-year probationary period for newly qualified drivers. If they receive six or more penalty points in their first two years after qualifying they will have their licence revoked and will have to take a new test. It will come into force on 2 June 1997.
■ Petrol must now be sold in litres rather than gallons.
■ MG launch the MGF.
■ Ascari Cars is founded, a British manufacturer of supercars named after the legendary Italian racing driver Alberto Ascari.
■ Rover launch their new 200 range.

JAGUAR XK8

By 1996, after twenty-one years, the XJS was getting long in the tooth and Jaguar needed a replacement. The XK8, with a 4-litre V8 engine, naturally aspirated or supercharged, replaced both the straight six HSE and the V12 XJS. The XK8 was the first of the new generation of Jaguars, which would grow to include the XF and the all new XJ. The first-generation XK8 shared its platform with the Aston Martin DB7, both in fact being derivatives of the ageing XJS. One significant revision was the use of the independent rear suspension from the XJ40. The naturally aspirated car, with 290bhp, was limited to 155mph and achieved 0–60 in 6.4 seconds, whilst the supercharged variant was limited to the same top speed, but with 370bhp was capable of 0–60 in 5.2 seconds.

LAND ROVER FREELANDER

In the late 1980s the market for compact SUVs was growing rapidly and market research by Land Rover suggested there was an opportunity in the sector. Initially Land Rover looked for a partner, but this came to nothing, so they decided to go it alone. At launch there were two variants: a five-door estate and a three-door 'semi convertible', with a choice of a 1.8-litre Rover K-series petrol engine or a 2.0-litre Rover L-series diesel engine. A V6 petrol variant came slightly later. After its launch in 1997 it became Europe's best-selling four-wheel-drive model until 2002. Since then the Freelander, like the Discovery, has 'grown up' into a more upmarket offering.

1996 From now on the driving test will include a theory test, which must be passed before the practical road test can be taken. The theory test replaces the previous questions on the Highway Code taken during the practical test.
■ Jaguar launch the XK8.
■ The second Severn Bridge is opened to relieve congestion on the first one. The second bridge becomes the default route into South Wales.

1997 The fitting of seat belts is made compulsory in all minibuses and coaches, both old and new, used to transport children.
■ Land Rover launch the Freelander.

The second Severn Crossing.

■ This year there are 3,599 deaths, 42,967 serious injuries and 327,544 minor injuries on British Roads.

■ Vickers puts Rolls-Royce up for sale to the highest bidder.

■ The 'dual notification' process is introduced for when a vehicle changes hands. This is the first major change concerning the sale and purchase of already registered cars for twenty years. It places the onus for informing the DVLA on the disposing keeper and requires both parties to provide details on the same form, the vehicle registration document. The disposer is responsible for ensuring both parties sign the document.

■ In March possibly the biggest motorway crash in British history occurs on the M42. An incredible 160 vehicles are involved when a lorry crashes into the back of a tanker as it comes off the slip road onto the motorway in fog. Three people are killed and 100 are injured.

■ The TX1 taxi, possibly the biggest single step forward in the history of London taxis, is launched. The design combines the unmistakable silhouette of the traditional taxi with huge advances in usability and refinement.

■ BRS Parcels, part of NFC PLC, is rebranded as Roadline and leaves NFC PLC by way of a management buyout and becomes Lynx Express Ltd.

1998 Four Star leaded petrol is withdrawn from all but a limited number of petrol stations, causing potential problems for owners of classic cars, who may have to rely on additives.

■ Rolls-Royce launches the Silver Seraph and Bentley launch the Mulsanne and Bentley Eight.

■ Rover announces its new 75.

■ Photocard driving licences are introduced, replacing the paper ones.

■ The Newbury bypass opens after many years of public debate and argument. Security during the building of the highly controversial scheme cost £30 million.

■ Britain's longest straight section of motorway opens, the A1(M) between Alconbury and Peterborough, where it is dead straight for 7 miles as it follows the route of the Roman Road, Ermine Street.

■ Rolls-Royce is split up into the two brands Rolls-Royce and Bentley. Volkswagen acquires Bentley, while BMW acquires the Rolls-Royce name.

■ The number of local licensing offices has now been reduced to forty.

■ The government announces that from 2001 the date component of car registrations would change every six months to reduce the buying rush for new cars in August. The plate format will also change significantly.

ROVER 75

The 75 was the first executive-sized car developed by Rover under BMW ownership. The 75 started life as part of a group of three designs proposed in the late '80s–early '90s for a large saloon, a small vehicle and a medium-sized executive-style car, which became the 75. Originally it was proposed to build on the existing 600 platform, but following the BMW takeover and the availability of more funding, it was decided to develop a totally new car. It would be produced with a range of petrol and diesel engines from 1.8-litre four-cylinder K-series units to 2.5-litre quad-cam KV6s. Later, in 2001, a V8 version would appear as the MG ZT. With the collapse of Rover in 2005 the 75 disappeared, at least for a while. With the MG name and assets bought by the Nanjing Automobile Group, it is hoped the 75 in MG guise will return as, indeed, the MGF already has.

■ The Statutory Off Road Notification (SORN) is introduced. If a vehicle is not taxed the keeper must declare it as being 'off road'.
■ Noble Cars is founded to manufacturer an entirely new domestically produced supercar.

1999 The Highway Code is revised and updated yet again.
■ Local authorities are given the power to impose 20mph limits on any local road without requiring the approval of the Secretary of State.
■ A White Paper is issued by HM Government called 'A New Deal for Transport – Better for Everyone'. We hope it will be!
■ The vehicle excise duty for cars of 1,100cc or less is reduced from £155 to £100 to encourage smaller, more economical and less polluting cars.
■ The M4 bus lane opens between Heathrow Airport and London at a cost of £1.9 million – and much controversy.
■ Volvo sells its car division to Ford but continues making trucks.
■ Aston Martin, now fully owned by Ford, becomes part of Ford's Premier Automotive Group, joining Jaguar, Lincoln and Volvo.
■ The first Severn Bridge gains Grade 1 listed status.
■ There is a trial of a fuel-cell powered taxis in London.
■ NFC PLC sells Pickfords to Allied Van Lines.
■ Deliveries of the Rover 75 begin.

The controversial M4 bus lane.

Learning to Cope with the Strain

Since 2000 the most significant start-up has been the new Mini in 2001, although two old marques – Connaught and Invicta – were briefly revived in 2004.

In terms of losses, however, some big names disappeared: Rover in 2005, MG in 2010 and Reliant in 2002. The specialist sports car maker Marcos also closed down in 2007. Rover and MG may yet rise again under the new Chinese ownership.

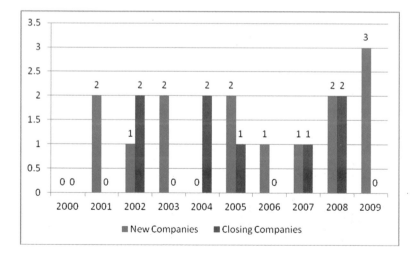

2000 The completion of the M60 makes Manchester the third British city encircled by a motorway, after London and Birmingham.

■BMW splits Rover into three. It retains the right to use the Mini name, sells Land Rover to Ford and the reminder, including MG and Rover, are sold to the Phoenix Group for £1.

■Ford announces it is to stop car production at Dagenham after sixty-eight years. Engine production will continue, both for Ford and (for the time being at least) Jaguar.

■HGV drivers and farmers blockade oil refineries in protest at fuel prices and duties. Panic buying ensues and petrol stations run out of fuel.

■General Motors announces a plan to close the Vauxhall car plant at Luton, with the loss of 2,000 jobs.

Ford Dagenham.

NEW MINI

When BMW purchased the Rover Group in 1994 from British Aerospace it also acquired the rights to use the name Mini for a car. The original Mini had survived until 2000, little changed in appearance from the first 1959 car. It was so well loved, BMW thought they would 'cash in' on this sentiment and launch a 'new' Mini – to be called MINI. Words like 'cynical marketing' do rather spring to mind, however. Although the new car does bear a slight passing resemblance to the original Mini – perhaps after a course of strong steroids – that is where the resemblance stops. The new car is 20 per cent longer, 70 per cent heavier, has an engine between 65 per cent and 89 per cent larger and costs a minimum of £12,000, whereas the Mini's 1959 price of £375 equates to just £7,500 today.

Jaguar X-type.

A London bendy bus.

■ Drink driving rehabilitation courses are adopted nationwide.
■ Morgan announce the radically 'different' Aero 8.
■ NFC PLC merges with Ocean Group PLC to become Excel PLC.

2001 Ultra-low-sulphur fuel goes on sale.
■ The new Mini is announced by BMW.
■ Rolls-Royce production is moved from Derby to a factory next to the old racing circuit at Goodwood.
■ The new licence plate is introduced, restoring the geographical link to the place of first registration. The format is two letters denoting place of registration, two numbers denoting the year of manufacture and three random letters.
■ Jaguar announce the X-type, which is the first of their cars to be made with four-wheel drive and a transverse engine, based on the Ford Mondeo platform.

2002 Drivers convicted of causing death by driving under the influence of alcohol or drugs are now required to pass an extended test before being allowed to drive again.
■ Vauxhall production at Luton ceases after ninety-seven years.
■ AA roadside phone boxes are scrapped, but a small number of wooden 'sentry' boxes are retained due to their listed status. The mobile phone has rendered them unnecessary.
■ The Police Reform Act 2002 provides for certain police duties to be undertaken by civilian police community support officers, including, most significantly, enforcement of parking restrictions. 'Traffic warden' as a title disappears.

ROLLS-ROYCE PHANTOM

The new Phantom was the first model introduced by Rolls-Royce under BMW ownership, and was intended to revive the glory of the earlier Phantoms as the pinnacle of automotive luxury. Although the days of coachbuilding have long passed, each Phantom is finished to individual customer specification at the dedicated Goodwood factory. The Phantom was originally going to have a tailor-made V16 engine, but the plan changed to using a BMW V12 instead. A handful of V16 Phantoms were made, one of which features in the film *Johnny English*, staring Rowan Atkinson. The 6.75-litre V12 unit delivers 453bhp, enough to give the Phantom sports car performance, with 149mph and 0–60 in 5.7 seconds being possible.

- The TXII taxi emerges onto London streets.
- Rolls-Royce Phantom production starts at Goodwood for delivery in 2003.
- Bendy buses appear in London.

2003 Jaguar launch the X350 version of the XJ, the first volume production car in the world to have chassis and bodywork made entirely of aluminium glued and riveted together.

- The congestion charge is introduced in London.
- The use of mobile phones when driving becomes a criminal offence.
- Britain's first toll motorway is opened, the M6 toll.
- The first Rolls-Royce Phantoms are delivered.
- The first 'red route' outside London is introduced on Stratford Road in Solihull.
- Bentley Continental GT is launched.
- The City Rover is launched. It is a rebadged Tata Indica made in Pune, India.

BENTLEY CONTINENTAL GT

When developing the Phaeton, intended to be the most luxurious car in the world, VW developed a novel W12 engine. The Phaeton in W12 guise was a marketing disaster and although the V6 diesel-engined version sold quite well, overall the production line never ran at over 25 per cent capacity. However, all was not lost, as the floorpan and engine found a home in a new Bentley model, the Continental GT. With four-wheel drive, twin turbos and 560bhp it could reach 60mph in 4.8 seconds and go on to 198mph. People will pay £150,000 for a VW called a Bentley, but not £90,000 for a VW called a VW!

2004 British car production reaches its highest level for five years.

■ Jaguar cease production in Coventry and move to Castle Bromwich into the old Spitfire/Lancaster factory.

■ Edinburgh considers and then rejects London-style congestion charging.

■ The last Motor Show at the NEC is held before it moves back to London in 2006.

■ The Aston Martin Volante is launched.

■ 20 per cent of households now have three or more cars.

■ The total number of motoring offences exceeds 13 million, a record.

■ TVR is bought by Russian Nikolay Smolensky.

■ The Jaguar E-type has a special exhibition devoted to it at London's Design Museum, forty years after it was launched.

■ The maximum penalty for causing death by driving under the influence of alcohol or drugs is increased to fourteen years.

■ A new style of registration certificate (VSC) is introduced to comply with a European directive to harmonise the certificates across the EU.

2005 The Rover Group files for bankruptcy. Also, it is the start of recriminations over the role of the Phoenix Group when they bought the remnants of BL from BMW.

■ The last Routemaster bus is retired from London's streets, with the exception of a few 'heritage' routes.

■ Britain's widest motorway section opens – the twelve-lane stretch of the M25 between J14 and J15. The section between J12 and J14 is a mere ten lanes wide.

■ The MG assets are bought by the Chinese Nanjing Automobile Group, with a view to reviving production of the Rover 75 and MGF.

■ Aston Martin begin production of the V8 Vantage, with a Jaguar-based engine. It will be their 'economy' model.

■ TVR finally closes shop after just a short period under Russian ownership.

■ There are now 612 'red light' cameras at traffic lights in Britain, of which 225 are in London.

■ Evidential breath tests can now be conducted at the roadside.

■ The Highways Agency issues a new policy, Interim Advice Note 60/05, recommending the use of concrete central barriers (as shown on p.155) in order to reduce the risk of crossover incidents on central reservations of motorways with high traffic levels. The policy states that in most cases, when concrete barriers are struck, they do not need to be repaired or need as much regular maintenance as steel barriers, therefore minimising the exposure and risk to road workers.

Aston Martin V8 Vantage.

■Significant new investment is announced in British car production. BMW will create 1,200 more jobs to make the new Mini at Cowley, Honda create 700 new jobs and Nissan announce plans to increase capacity and build the Qashqai in Sunderland.

2006 The M42 becomes the first motorway where the use of the hard shoulder is permitted during peak hours.
■Britain's first motorway car-share lane is announced on the M606/M62 at J26, where a special lane is created for cars carrying more than one person, allowing traffic to bypass congestion.
■Lotus announces a totally new mid-engined car, which will be released in about two years.
■The 1.5 millionth car emerges from Honda at Bridgend.
■Cardiff now has Britain's worst rush hour for congestion, the average commuter being delayed by thirty minutes and thirteen seconds, compared to the national average of twenty-two minutes.
■The maximum charge for an MoT test increases by £6.20 to £50.35.
■The Chancellor delays any increase in fuel duty for at least six months.
■The Motor Show returns to London at its new location, the Excel Centre.
■The Jaguar XK wins the Car of the Year award.

■Aston Martin produce their 30,000th car.

■The first widespread use of Automatic Number Plate Recognition (ANPR) technology takes place by police forces throughout the country.

■A Gatso speed camera installed at a temporary 50mph limit in roadworks on the M62 at Ferrybridge catches 18,000 people in eighteen months and raises a record £1million.

■The TX4 is the latest taxi model to be approved for use as a licensed London taxi.

■Digital tachographs become compulsory on appropriate vehicles.

2007 Bentley announce their fastest ever car, the £137,500 GT Speed. Its top speed is well over 200mph and 0–60 takes 4.3 seconds.

■Lewis Hamilton is runner-up in the F1 championship in his first competitive year.

■Sheila Thompson, aged 105, loses her no-claims discount for the first time after seventy-one years of fault-free motoring when she has a minor collision with a parked car.

2008 Tata takes over Jaguar-Land Rover from Ford, with a commitment to invest heavily in new models.

■The new Roewe 550 is launched in Shanghai, with hopes of returning production to the MG factory.

■The AA introduce patrols on motorcycles and electric bikes in London to avoid congestion.

■20 per cent of cars are now failing the MoT test.

■Comprehensive breath testing statistics are collected by machines that store results for transfer to a central database.

2009 Jaguar release the all new XJ.

■The withdrawal of bendy buses from London's streets begins.

■The government announces an incentive scheme to help people buy electric cars. This amounts to a £5,000 subsidy.

■Car colours stage a return to the 'acid' colours of the 1970s, and white is definitely 'out'.

■The government announces the car scrappage scheme, whereby any car which is over 10 years old and has been in a person's possession for at least twelve months will attract a payment of £1,000 from the government and a discount of £1,000 from a manufacturer towards the purchase of a new car.

JAGUAR XJ

In 2009 Jaguar launched the third of its new product range, a totally new XJ. This new luxury saloon was at the leading edge of chassis design, featuring not just an all-alloy body shell, but also an all aluminium frame which was entirely riveted and bonded together, making it considerably lighter than its main competitors – the Mercedes S Class, Audi A8 and Lexus 450. With a choice of engines ranging from a 3-litre V6 diesel to a supercharged 5-litre V8 petrol and a choice of standard or long wheelbase, Jaguar again had a winner.

2010 A report by Department of Transport recommends reducing the drink drive limit to 50mg.

■ Rolls-Royce launch the Ghost, presented as a 'more affordable' and smaller version of the Phantom, costing 'only' £170,000. It has a similar 6.6-litre twin-turbo V12 to the Phantom.

■ The Department of Transport recommends a speed limit of 65mph for all vehicles capable of carrying eight or more people.

■ Aston Martin revive the Rapide name on a four-door car, but not using the Lagonda name.

Rolls-Royce Ghost.

■ The 'Boris' bike scheme appears in London, although it really should be called the Barclays scheme after its sponsor.

■ The government's scrappage scheme is extended for three months into 2010.

2011 Hammersmith Flyover is closed on 23 December because of corrosion in the post-tensioned steel cables resulting from salt used to prevent icing. It is reopened on 13 January 2012 for a single lane in each direction. Repairs will extend the life of the flyover by about fifteen years, when it may be replaced by a tunnel.

■ In November a massive crash on the M5 near Taunton is blamed on fog, possibly made worse by bonfire night smoke. Seven people are killed and fifty-one injured when a huge fireball engulfed the scene.

■ The last bendy buses are withdrawn in London.

Right: Hindhead Tunnel.

- Morgan announce an all-new three wheeler.
- Aston Martin launch the curious Cygnet, basically a Toyota iQ in fancy dress and costing twice as much, £30,995 for the 'base' model. Oh, and you have to already own an Aston Martin in order to gain the privilege of paying 'twice' for a Toyota.
- The Hindhead Tunnel on the A3 opens, the longest non-estuary road tunnel in Britain (1.14 miles). Finally, the whole of the London–Portsmouth road is a dual carriageway.

2012 700,000 jobs in Britain now rely on the car industry.
- Nissan is now the UK's largest producer of cars.
- The new Routemaster bus begins operating in London.
- The worst ever speeding offence occurs, with a 65-mile chase of a stolen Audi RS5 at speeds of up to 180mph.
- Jaguar launch the XF Sportbrake, their first estate car.
- JLR launch the new all aluminium Range Rover, a world first for a 4x4 off-road car.
- JLR also announce the totally new 'baby' Range Rover, the Evoque.
- Clamping cars on private land is prohibited, unless by bailiffs under a county court judgment.
- The M4 bus lane is scrapped, having been deemed a disastrous failure.
- On one day during the Olympics a record 47,105 'Boris' bikes are rented.

RANGE ROVER EVOQUE
The Evoque represents a departure for Land Rover. For the first time they have marketed a second distinct product under the Range Rover name, a 'baby' Range Rover aimed at the 'compact' SUV market. With unitary construction, only four cylinder engines, options of two-or four-wheel drive and no transfer box, it is radically different from both the existing Range Rover and the Discovery and Freelander. But the dramatic styling and luxurious interior have won praise and even in its first year of production Land Rover sold 88,000 units – the waiting list is still around nine months.

■ Due to 'technical issues' and the fact that the new digital cameras have not yet been legally authorised, not a single speeding ticket is issued in 2012 by any of the speed cameras on the M25.

■ Two 1960s petrol station canopies gain listed status: the sweeping concrete canopy at Markham Moor off the A1 and one on the A6 at Red Hill in Leicestershire.

■ Britain's oldest driver is 105-year-old Harry Jamieson, who got his first licence in 1924 aged 17. Since then he has covered more than 2 million miles. He currently drives a 1980s Ford Escort, slightly smaller than the Rolls-Royce Silver Ghost armoured car he learned to drive in. Oh, and he's never had a point on his licence!

■ A million drivers are now aged over 80.

■ Manganese Bronze, the manufacturer of most London black cabs, hits serious financial problems as a result of a large recall. It looks possible the business may be bought by the Chinese.

■ The government announces that from 2013 insurance companies may no longer include gender as a factor in setting insurance premiums.

■ TVR finally goes out of business.